THE UNSUNG YEARS
My Youth 1930–1945

Lisbeth Fischer Leicht

MINERVA PRESS

LONDON

MONTREUX   LOS ANGELES   SYDNEY

THE UNSUNG YEARS
Copyright © Lisbeth Fischer Leicht 1997

All Rights Reserved

ISBN 1 86106 492 6

First published 1997 by
MINERVA PRESS
195 Knightsbridge
London SW7 1RE

Printed in Great Britain by
Biddles Ltd, Kings Lynn, Norfolk

To Margaret

THE UNSUNG YEARS
My Youth 1930–1945

affectionately

Lisl

For my children and grandchildren

The original text of this book is in the hands of Vienna University where the 'Documentation of Biographical Records' within the Institute for Economic and Social History deals in one section specifically with Jewish personal histories of the period. It was founded for a relevant research project and has formed the basis for a number of scientific publications. In responding to the book, the university refers to the ambivalent attitude of Austria to its past and expresses the wish and hope that this autobiography will be published in Austria also and would find a readership in the German language. To quote from their appraisal, it will provide 'a further tessera in the mosaic of the essential work of remembrance'.

The original letters included in this book are being preserved in the archives of the Institute of Contemporary History and Wiener Library in London where they are made available to researchers and *bona fide* students of the period.

Contents

Foreword

September 1994

For some time now the germ of an idea has lain dormant in my mind, that I should write the memoirs of my childhood and adolescence: then my grandchildren might be able to colour in, as it were, the pages of history they will learn in the course of their studies which may appear, as so often is the case, not to have any bearing on their own lives and circumstances. The history books they will read will undoubtedly provide them with all the relevant dates and basic facts that are of interest, and I could never hope to be as accurate and precise in that respect, nor would I wish to give a truly historical account of what happened in the 1930s and the 1940s even if I were capable of doing so. What I would like to do, though, is to give impressions of a childhood in Vienna in those turbulent years that saw the rise of fascism in Europe, a rise that so many could not, or would note, take seriously until it was too late.

It is usually more difficult to see and understand clearly what goes on in one's own contemporary world than to judge events and developments in retrospect. In particular, it is difficult to concern oneself with trends or troubles if these do not directly affect one: there is, after all, only one life and there is so much to do! However, the small injustices of today become the big transgressions of tomorrow. Democratic freedoms and rights need to be defended fearlessly at all times lest they become eroded, until once again the indifference and carelessness of a people result in the calamity of totalitarian oppression.

In the pages that follow, then, I will try to speak of the experiences which have shaped my life, influenced my thinking and which must inevitably have had some bearing on the way I brought up my children. I would like to believe that what I am going to tell them of my background, which is part of their heritage also, may affect their attitudes and actions and make them into more complete human beings.

Speaking of the art of conducting an orchestra, Eugene Goossens (a member of the distinguished family of musicians and instrument builders) is reputed to have said there were only two difficulties: how to start and how to finish. I rather think this will be my predicament also. I will begin with my early childhood and sketch in the events of those momentous times which brought me to this country in February 1939, before the outbreak of the Second World War in the September of that year.

Chapter One
My Childhood Years

I have always regretted not knowing a great deal of my paternal grandparents and so, being denied knowing them as people of flesh and blood, unable to picture their lives, their hopes and fears, I have never succeeded in establishing a link with them in my imagination. I only know the outline of their existence, their dates of birth and death and where these took place.

On my mother's side, the grandparents Pollak featured considerably in my young life. Grandfather Leopold was born in Nikolsburg, Moravia, in 1851 and grandmother Bertha (née Fischer) was born in Pohrlitz, Moravia, in 1855. This region was at that time in the Austro-Hungarian Empire, but since the First World War had become part of Czechoslovakia. Grosspapa (as Austrian children called their grandfather) and Grossmama lived in the flat at the top of our house and I was a frequent visitor there. After grandfather died Grossmama came to live with us, and the furniture in our flat was moved around so as to accommodate a small part of hers. These were large, solid pieces in the main, and were used for her own separate room where she spent much of her time, some in devout prayer, for, though not orthodox, my grandparents observed all the Jewish religious laws and central to these was the Sabbath, of course.

She stayed with us until after the *Anschluss* when it became imperative she was found a safe haven, with the rest of the family feverishly trying to emigrate from Hitler's new Austria. At that time Czechoslovakia, where my uncle and his family lived, was still considered 'safe' – though as history showed it was not to be for long – and the old lady was fetched and taken by car to Rohatec, not far from the border. I never saw her again.

Though overshadowed by my father's illness and his death when I was twelve years old, my childhood was happy. School was probably among the most important factors. Like all Austrian children I started primary school at six, and for me it was a short walk up our street and round the corner where a friendly, most competent teacher reigned supreme. The children came from all kinds of backgrounds; some spoke the language correctly, others spoke a Viennese dialect, understood by all and often used colloquially, though probably only within the family. One naughty, recalcitrant boy, when exasperated by his lack of success at his work, used outrageously racy language, for which misdemeanour he often had to stand in the corner, but was regarded by the rest of the class with a certain respect for his bravery in uttering the unspeakable words.

School was synonymous with enjoyment, reading and writing a delight; the old wooden desks bore the marks of generations of pupils' use and abuse; the inkwells had to be cleaned and refilled periodically and only those who were well-behaved and dependable were allowed the privilege of such tasks. School started at eight o'clock and finished at one, and then home to the midday meal. It was the main meal of the day shared by all the family, though my father, who was often absent in those early days and later, when he was in hospital for long periods, was seldom there at all. His work in the newspaper world, both in editorial and advertising departments of publications such as *Der Tag* and *Die Bühne*, was frequently interrupted by ill health. As a result his income was variable and often greatly depressed, but mother's gift for keeping house and producing good, wholesome food from simple ingredients meant that my brother and I never felt in any way deprived. Now and then my brother Peter, four years my senior, and I might be given ten *Groschen* to buy and share a bar of chocolate; I don't recall ever in my childhood eating a bar of chocolate by myself.

Once a week my mother's sister, my beloved Aunt Adele, came to our flat to have lunch. These were red letter days indeed. She worked as personal assistant to the president of the Austrian Sugar Industry and had much contact with the great and the good in that milieu. Being a born raconteur, or should I say raconteuse, she regaled us with stories and *bon mots* which we found vastly entertaining, such as the pronouncement of one cynical colleague that there were two sorts of people in the world, the ones you would not touch with a barge pole and the others you would only touch with a barge pole. She and her husband, my father's brother Hermann, were childless and, as they were both working, relatively affluent. These visits also meant special treats, for she brought oranges and bananas, luxuries that were not normally to be seen in our home.

Now and then there were school outings, a tram ride beyond the suburbs and out into the countryside, the Wienerwald, a pleasant region of rolling hills and woodland. We carried small rucksacks with the day's provisions and ran and played, oblivious of the civil unrest and political agitation which would ultimately lead to turmoil and terror.

At home, life was still calm and uneventful. I loved running upstairs to see our grandparents. Grandfather had a gift with young children and could amuse me without the aid of toys and other artefacts, merely by talking to me in a language of his own devising, totally unrelated to any real language, and getting me to respond in similar fashion. It was much better than fairy stories. Sometimes, after we had played our games sitting in the kitchen, he would make toast on the solid surface of the kitchen range and rub it with a little garlic. This was called *Panetz* and I thought it delicious.

Always welcome in my grandparents' home, I was free to see the many fascinating things they possessed: some old Bohemian glass, the chiming grandfather clock, the tall chest of drawers where the remains of their stationers' shop were kept. This was because they had come to live in Vienna – it must have been around 1880 – after Grandfather had lost a large part of his patrimony in a disastrous financial crisis of devaluation in the country. With what could be salvaged from their funds they purchased a shop and made a meagre living, as Grandfather, though a scholar of Hebrew and the classics, was no businessman and I do believe that it was Grandmother who, by her thrift and general good management and housekeeping, kept the family going.

Sometimes, after she had finished the morning's chores of cleaning and preparing the midday meal and had washed herself, Grandmother might let me keep her company while in front of the mahogany-framed mirror she would arrange her long hair, combed and brushed carefully, piled neatly on top of the head with a little parting to the front. She might then later let me watch her in the kitchen, which interested me greatly, as she was a wonderful cook and I have never tasted the equal of her feathery sponge cakes. If ever Peter or I were ill she would come downstairs and present us with one of these confections, which contributed to a rapid recovery!

Looking back at their lives I marvel at my grandparents' modesty and their evident ability to find happiness without the luxuries that are nowadays taken for granted. Grandmother would show the greatest pleasure and appreciation of the gift of a hand-knitted scarf for her birthday; I remember its shape to this day – a triangle with a motif of stripes in muted colours, principally grey, black and white. In common with most of her contemporaries she never wore bright colours; the rule was black for everyday and grey for special occasions, a decorative choker round the throat and a ormolu-type brooch pinned to her bosom. Grandfather was equally undemanding; he might receive pulse-warmers, as they were called, for a present. These were to keep his hands from getting too chilled. Their contentedness sprang from an inner strength and faith, not the outward trappings of material possessions.

When they celebrated their golden wedding my grandparents danced a polka to the acclamation of all those assembled. This was the last time that virtually all the members of our family congregated in the flat before the general dispersal after 1938. It was a moving occasion with the kind of warmth and emotion so typical of Jewish family life. There was punch – if I am not mistaken it was based on tea and contained only a modicum of alcohol! Toasts were proposed and speeches were made and the children all recited poems suited to this special anniversary. The deputy mayor of Vienna called with a colleague to present the good wishes of the City of Vienna in person and brought a gift of a handsomely crafted leather box, engraved in gold, and a commemorative scroll.

It is only in retrospect that I have come to regard as a great void the lack of knowledge of my paternal grandparents, the details of their circumstances and way of life, owing to the fact that they died young, leaving their children orphaned so that my father would not himself have remembered them clearly. From the now faded and almost crumbling old birth certificates I have in my possession all I know is that my father's father, Carl Leicht, was born in Simmering, a suburb of Vienna, in 1853. He was a master shoemaker and he and his wife Ernestine (née Götzlinger) lived in Hernals, Vienna, where my father Ludwig was born in 1889. Carl and Ernestine died in an influenza epidemic and their children (my father Ludwig, his brother Hermann and their sister Emilie) were brought up by an aunt. My father was a boy of only eight or nine when his parents died. The aunt must have been a long-suffering lady, having to deal with two lively boys and a girl.

Conversely I realise how deep and lasting have been the impressions made on me so very early in life by my maternal grandparents: their mode of life and religious worship within their home. These memories are still relatively fresh. For instance the celebration of the Passover, preceded by a general kind of spring-cleaning which included bringing out the 'best' china, washing each and every utensil to be used. This was in readiness for the ceremony of the Seder, a service in the home presided over by the father, or in this case the grandfather, who led the prayers in remembrance of the exodus from Egypt. In the course of the festive meal, which features symbolically unleavened bread and bitter herbs, the youngest child in the family asks the question, 'Why is this night different from all other nights?' and the answer is the long biblical story of the Jews' release from bondage and of delivery.

My grandparents' social life was very limited indeed, but they were on friendly terms with their neighbour on the floor below them, an old lady with snow-white hair and lovely features. She would go up to them for a chat – she was widowed, her husband had been an officer in the old Austro-Hungarian Army. A devout Catholic, she could be seen early every morning going to mass. The matter of their different religions did not interfere with their pleasant relationship; on the contrary they respected one another's beliefs and appeared free from prejudice on either side.

I was of course too young then for them to talk to me of the historical events which had taken place in Vienna in the course of their lives, but even from odd passing remarks I gathered that they had held the Habsburg monarchy in great esteem. This impression has since been reinforced by my coming across, among papers which have ended up in my possession, a pamphlet published in celebration of the Fiftieth Jubilee of his reign of the Emperor Franz Joseph on 24th June 1898. There is also a similarly produced tract on the tragic assassination of his wife, the Empress Elisabeth, on the 10th September of the same year, in which tribute is paid to the murdered Empress and the Emperor expresses his thanks to his people for their love and sympathy. These documents are reproduced on the following pages.

It may well be that my grandparents' feelings towards Franz Joseph were coloured by the fact that the monarch opposed the election of Karl Lueger to the office of Burgomaster of Vienna; he was a rabid anti-Semite,[*] who as a shrewd politician used anti-Semitism to curry favour with the population and thereby gain power. It cannot be denied, however, that Lueger did much for Vienna.

I had known that grandfather had heart trouble and remember the small brown bottle containing digitalis, which, dispensed on lumps of sugar, he took as a remedy at certain times. There were frequent occasions when my mother was called in the middle of the night to help Grandmother with the old gentleman, then over eighty, suffering minor heart attacks. It was not altogether a surprise when he died in 1932 or possibly 1933, but I was sad and shocked to see the coffin, a plain wooden one according to Jewish law, carried out of the house. It struck me as odd that one so beloved should be consigned to the desolate grounds of a cemetery. I rather fancied the idea of installing the coffin on top of the piano.

In stark contrast to the simplicity of the Jewish funeral was that of a neighbour who had lived in the house opposite ours. He was taken to his last resting-place in a splendid glass coach drawn by horses bedecked with black plumes and other finery, with flowers piled high round the coffin, which was draped with black and mauve silks. I watched this spectacle from our windows, enthralled but at the same time terrified. This, it was explained to me, was a Catholic funeral. I found it impressive, to say the least.

Amongst some of my earliest recollections, and a very delightful one, though little more than a faint cameo in the memory, is a ride in an open horse-drawn trap along a country lane lined with rowan trees, with the red berries and delicate fronds brushing against my face. This memorable outing must have taken place when we were on holiday not far from Vienna, staying in rooms rented for a few weeks, where my father could come and join us at weekends. This is a time I only dimly recall and must have been before he was taken ill with tuberculosis and had to be away from us so often, either in hospital or

---

[*] See 'Fin-de-Siècle Vienna', *Politics and Culture* by Carl E. Schorske, Cambridge University Press, pp.133–4.

ZUR ERINNERUNG

AN DEN

AUS ANLASS DES FÜNFZIGJÄHRIGEN REGIERUNGS-JUBILÄUMS

S^{R.} MAJESTÄT DES KAISERS FRANZ JOSEPH I.

AM

24. JUNI 1898

VERANSTALTETEN

KINDER-HULDIGUNGS-FESTZUG.

ALLEN THEILNEHMERN GEWIDMET

VON DER

K. K. REICHS-HAUPT- UND RESIDENZSTADT WIEN.

Ansprache des Bürgermeisters.

Vorbeimarsch der Knaben.

Erwiderung Sr. Majestät.

Vorbeimarsch der Mädchen.

Ansprache des Bürgermeisters:

Eure kaiserliche und königliche Apostolische Majestät! Allergnädigster Kaiser und Herr!

Es ist nicht ein prunkvoller Festzug, der heute vor Eurer Majestät vorüberziehen wird, es sind nicht die Mächtigen der Erde, welche heute Eurer Majestät huldigen werden, aber es ist das kostbarste Gut, welches die Wiener ihrem Herrn und Kaiser vorweisen können: es sind die Kinder des Volkes. Sie sind es, welche Bürgen sind für jetzt und für die Zukunft. Aus den jubelnden Zurufen derselben mögen Eure Majestät den Ruf der Treue für jetzt und für die Zukunft hören. Aus den jubelnden Zurufen der Kinder mag für jedermann hervorgehen: Österreich wird ewig stehen. So wie die Eltern ihre Kinder zu den Großeltern führen, damit letztere aus der Liebe der Enkel die fortdauernde Liebe der Kinder erkennen, so führen wir heute die Kinder zu ihrem Kaiser, damit sie Zeugen sind für ihre Eltern. Und der heutige Tag wird all den Kindern unvergesslich bleiben; noch in fernen Jahren wird ihnen in Erinnerung sein, dass sie Gelegenheit hatten, dem Kaiser zu danken, der so viel für sein Reich geschaffen, so viel für die Stadt Wien gethan hat. Noch in fernen Jahren wird als ihre angenehmste und schönste Erinnerung aus ihrer Kindheit in ihnen der Ruf nachklingen, den wir jetzt Alle begeistert ausbringen: Seine Majestät, unser allergnädigster Kaiser und Herr, er lebe hoch!

Antwort Seiner Majestät des Kaisers:

Selten bin Ich einer Einladung gerührteren Herzens gefolgt, als der heutigen. Sind es doch die Kinder des Volkes, das Innerste seines Herzens, die Mir heute näher treten, und in deren frischen Gefühlen und Eindrücken wir Alle das Bild und zugleich das Unterpfand für eine gedeihliche Zukunft mit Zuversicht erkennen.

Mögen die Kinder jetzt und fortan in Treue und Vertrauen zu ihrem Kaiser aufblicken, der ihnen, des Staates reicher Hoffnung, gleiches Vertrauen und ein stetes warmes Interesse zuwenden wird.

Jenen, welchen das schwere und verantwortungsvolle, aber heilige Amt der Schulerziehung obliegt, bringe Ich den berechtigten, dringenden Wunsch besorgter Eltern in Erinnerung, sie möchten sich der ihnen anvertrauten Aufgabe in ernster und liebevoller Arbeit widmen und dieselbe unbeirrt zu segensreichem Ende führen.

Ihnen Allen aber, Vertretern Meines lieben Wien, Eltern und Lehrern, die Sie Mir diesen schönen Tag bereitet haben, sage Ich von ganzem Herzen Meinen innigen und anerkennendsten Dank.

24.Dez.1837.
10.September 1898.

GEWIDMET VON DER K. K. REICHSHAUPT- UND RESIDENZSTADT WIEN.

UNSERE KAISERIN.

———

Niemals werden die Völker unseres schönen, großen Vaterlandes jenes Tages vergessen, der ihnen die entsetzlich erschütternde Kunde brachte von dem Hinscheiden der Kaiserin Elisabeth, der edlen Gemahlin unseres geliebten Kaisers Franz Joseph I.

Am 10. September 1898 wurde Kaiserin Elisabeth von Österreich in Genf ermordet, von einem ruchlosen, wahnwitzigen Verbrecher, der nur deshalb den Mordstahl gegen die edle Fürstin zückte, weil sie eine Krone trug, eine Krone, deren Glanz sie niemals blendete, die sie so gern abgelegt hätte, um nur ganz dem Schönen und Guten zu leben, dem reinen Genusse der Natur, den hehren Freuden, welche die Kunst einer edlen Menschenseele einflösst. Die dahingeschiedene Kaiserin hat von der Macht, mit der sie das Schicksal umkleidete, nie einen anderen Gebrauch gemacht, als den, wohlzuthun und Gutes zu stiften, wo und wie sie nur konnte.

Im bayerischen Schlosse Possenhofen am Starnbergersee, welches sich hinter dichten Baumkronen fast ganz verbirgt, erblickte Prinzessin Elisabeth Eugenie als zweitälteste Tochter des Herzogs Maximilian in Bayern und der Herzogin Ludovica am 24. December 1837 das Licht der Welt. Am heiligen Abend wurde sie in die Wiege gelegt, und der Herzog nannte sie deshalb sein liebes »Christkindel«.

In lieblicher Anmuth und Heiterkeit blühte sie empor, und als sie mit ihrer Mutter und ihrer älteren Schwester Helene, welche sich später mit dem Fürsten von Thurn und Taxis vermählte, im Sommer des Jahres 1853 zum Besuche ihrer erlauchten Tante, der Mutter unseres Kaisers, in Ischl weilte, da machte ihre zarte Schönheit, ihr frisches, munteres Wesen auf das Herz des Kaisers einen tiefen unauslöschlichen Eindruck.

»Herr Pfarrer, segnen Sie uns, das ist meine Braut,« sprach der Kaiser, als er Prinzessin Elisabeth in der Frühe des 19. August in die Kirche von Ischl führte.

Am 24. April 1854 fand in der Augustiner-Hofkirche in Wien die feierliche Trauung des Kaiserpaares statt. Am Vortage hatte Prinzessin Elisabeth ihren Einzug vom k. k. Theresianum in die Hofburg gehalten. Wien glich einem Blumengarten; die altersgrauen Mauern verschwanden hinter den lieblichen Blüten des Frühlings. Die schönste Rose war Elisabeth, aus dem Bayerlande in den Boden unseres Vaterlandes verpflanzt.

Und fortan blieb Kaiserin Elisabeth die treueste Tochter ihres neuen Vaterlandes, die hingebendste, liebevollste Gattin, die sorgsamste Mutter, die mit einer Liebe, wie sie nur das Mutterherz kennt, an ihren Kindern hieng.

Gottes unerforschlicher Rathschluss ließ sie an diesen viele Freude erleben, aber auch viel, unsäglich viel Leid.

Das erste Kind, welches der Himmel am 5. März 1855 dem Kaiserpaare schenkte, Erzherzogin Sophie, verschied schon im zartesten Kindesalter auf einer Reise der Majestäten in Ungarn, die sich von ihrem Lieblinge nicht trennen wollten. Am 12. Juli 1856 war die zweite Prinzessin, Erzherzogin Gisela, geboren worden, die zur Freude ihrer Eltern heranblühte und sich in dem Jubeljahre 1873, als der Kaiser sein fünfundzwanzigjähriges Herrscherjubiläum feierte, mit dem Prinzen Leopold von Bayern vermählte.

Der heißeste Wunsch der Kaiserin, ihrem erlauchten Gemahl den Erben des Thrones zu schenken, erfüllte sich zur innigsten Freude der Herrscherin, als am 21. August 1858 in dem kaiserlichen Lustschlosse Laxenburg, wo auch unser Kaiser heitere Tage der Kindheit verlebt hatte, Kronprinz Rudolf geboren wurde.

Welches Glück, welche Seligkeit bereitete der Kaiserin das Heranwachsen dieses Sohnes, die schöne Entfaltung seiner körperlichen und geistigen Vorzüge! Wie tief erschütterte sie der jähe Tod des Thronerben, den Gottes Wille am 30. Jänner 1889 von dieser Erde abrief!

Und doch hatte unsere edle Kaiserin in ihrem namenlosen Leide noch die Seelenstärke, in den Tagen dieses unfassbaren Schmerzes ihren kaiserlichen Gemahl aufzurichten, ihn zu trösten und zu stärken. Mochte ihr Mutterherz brechen, an dem Leben, an der Gesundheit des Kaisers hieng die Wohlfahrt Tausender, die Größe und das Glück des Reiches.

Damals sagte der Kaiser zu den Abgeordneten des österreichischen Reichsrathes: »Wie viel Ich in diesen schweren Tagen Meiner innigstgeliebten Frau, der Kaiserin, zu danken habe, welche große Stütze sie Mir gewesen ist, kann Ich nicht beschreiben, nicht warm genug aussprechen; Ich kann dem Himmel nicht genug danken, dass er Mir solch eine Lebensgefährtin gegeben hat.«

Wie lebensfroh, wie glücklich war die Kaiserin noch wenige Jahre vor dem Tode des Kronprinzen gewesen, als sie am 24. April 1879 mit ihrem erlauchten kaiserlichen Gemahl vor dem Altar der Votivkirche niederkniete, um die silberne Hochzeit zu feiern. Welche Fülle des Glückes schien dieser Tag zu verheißen, mit welcher Freude ließ die Kaiserin den zauberhaft schönen Festzug der Stadt Wien an sich vorüberziehen!

Welche Tage stillen Glückes verlebte die Kaiserin in ihrem schönen Lustschlosse Lainz, in dem prächtigen kaiserlichen Thiergarten bei Wien, sowie in ihrem lieben Ungarlande, seitdem sie am 8. Juni 1867 feierlich zur Königin Ungarns gekrönt worden war. In Ungarn war auch am 22. April 1868 Erzherzogin Marie Valerie geboren worden, an der das Herz der Kaiserin mit besonderer Liebe und Zärtlichkeit hieng.

In dem märchenhaft schönen Schlosse Achilleion auf Korfu, welches die Kaiserin sich erbauen ließ, und das sie so sehr liebte, erhebt sich, umkränzt von düsteren Cypressen, ein ergreifend schönes Denkmal, welches die schmerzgebeugte Mutter ihrem kaiserlichen Sohne, der ihres Herzens Hoffnungsstern gewesen war, errichten ließ.

Seit dem Tode des Kronprinzen hat die edle kaiserliche Dulderin das Glück stiller Herzensfreuden selten mehr empfunden. Auch der furchtbare Tod ihrer Schwester, der Herzogin Sophie von Alençon, die im Mai 1897 zu Paris in den Flammen umkam, erschütterte die Kaiserin aufs tiefste.

Sie suchte auf Reisen Zerstreuung; es zog sie nach dem sonnigen Süden, sie ließ die Wunder der Alpenwelt, die Pracht des Meeres an ihren entzückten Blicken vorübergleiten.

Aus den Schönheiten der Natur schöpfte sie Trost und Erquickung, in den Werken der Dichter und Künstler suchte ihr edler Geist Erhebung, und die Tröstungen der Religion senkten in dieses schwergeprüfte Fürstenherz den Frieden, der nur vom Himmel kommt und nicht von dieser Erde ist.

Die Nachricht von dem Tode der Kaiserin hatte in der ganzen Monarchie und besonders in der Kaiserstadt an der Donau die tiefste Theilnahme erregt. Wien war buchstäblich in Trauer gehüllt, alle Freude in der lebensfrohen Kaiserstadt war erstorben; von allen Häusern flatterten die schwarzen Fahnen — der letzte Gruß, den die treuen Wiener ihrer todten Kaiserin boten.

Verwelkt sind schon all die prachtvollen Blumenkränze, welche den Sarg der großen und edlen Fürstin in der Kaisergruft zu Wien schmückten, aber unverwelklich ist der Kranz inniger Liebe und Dankbarkeit, den die Völker Österreich-Ungarns für alle Zeiten ihrer innigstgeliebten Kaiserin und Königin weihen werden.

Der Dank des Kaisers.

Se. Majestät hat nachstehendes Allerhöchstes Handschreiben erlassen:

Lieber Graf Thun! In den Tagen unermesslicher Trauer, in welche der Heimgang Meiner gottseligen Gemahlin, Ihrer Majestät der Kaiserin und Königin Elisabeth, Mich und Mein Haus versetzte, hat sich die Liebe und Theilnahme Meiner Völker, sowie die Pietät für die Verblichene in rührender und erhebender Weise geäußert.

Ich folge dem Zuge Meines Herzens, indem Ich Sie beauftrage, die beifolgende unmittelbar an Meine geliebten Völker gerichtete Danksagung in entsprechender Weise zu veröffentlichen.

Schönbrunn, am 16. September 1898.

Franz Joseph *m. p.*   Thun *m. p.*

AN MEINE VÖLKER!

Die schwerste, grausamste Prüfung hat Mich und Mein Haus heimgesucht.

Meine Frau, die Zierde Meines Thrones, die treue Gefährtin, die Mir in den schwersten Stunden Meines Lebens Trost und Stütze war — an der Ich mehr verloren habe, als Ich auszusprechen vermag, ist nicht mehr. Ein entsetzliches Verhängnis hat Sie Mir und Meinen Völkern entrissen.

Eine Mörderhand, das Werkzeug des wahnwitzigen Fanatismus, der die Vernichtung der bestehenden gesellschaftlichen Ordnung sich zum Ziele setzt, hat sich gegen die edelste der Frauen erhoben und in blindem, ziellosem Hass das Herz getroffen, das keinen Hass gekannt und nur für das Gute geschlagen hat.

Mitten in dem grenzenlosen Schmerze, der Mich und Mein Haus erfasst, angesichts der unerhörten That, welche die ganze gesittete Welt in Schaudern versetzt, dringt zunächst die Stimme Meiner geliebten Völker lindernd zu Meinem Herzen. Indem ich Mich der göttlichen Fügung, die so Schweres und Unfassbares über Mich verhängt, in Demuth beuge, muss Ich der Vorsehung Dank sagen für das hohe Gut, das Mir verblieben; für die Liebe und Treue der Millionen, die in der Stunde des Leidens Mich und die Meinen umgibt.

In tausend Zeichen, von nah und fern, von hoch und nieder, hat sich der Schmerz und die Trauer um die gottselige Kaiserin und Königin geäußert. In rührendem Zusammenklang ertönt die Klage Aller über den unermesslichen Verlust als getreuer Wiederhall dessen, was Meine Seele bewegt.

Wie Ich das Gedächtnis Meiner heißgeliebten Gemahlin heilig halte bis zur letzten Stunde, so bleibt Ihr in der Dankbarkeit und Verehrung Meiner Völker ein unvergängliches Denkmal für alle Zeiten errichtet.

Aus den Tiefen Meines bekümmerten Herzens danke Ich Allen für dieses neue Pfand hingebungsvoller Theilnahme.

Wenn die Festklänge, welche dieses Jahr begleiten sollten, verstummen müssen, so bleibt Mir die Erinnerung an die zahllosen Beweise von Anhänglichkeit und warmem Mitgefühl die wertvollste Gabe, welche Mir dargebracht werden konnte.

Die Gemeinsamkeit unseres Schmerzes schlingt ein neues, inniges Band um Thron und Vaterland. Aus der unwandelbaren Liebe Meiner Völker schöpfe Ich nicht nur das verstärkte Gefühl der Pflicht, auszuharren in der Mir gewordenen Sendung, sondern auch die Hoffnung des Gelingens.

Ich bete zu dem Allmächtigen, der Mich so schwer heimgesucht, dass Er Mir noch Kraft gebe, zu erfüllen, wozu Ich berufen bin. Ich bete, dass Er Meine Völker segne und erleuchte, den Weg der Liebe und Eintracht zu finden, auf dem sie gedeihen und glücklich werden mögen.

Schönbrunn, am 16. September 1898.

Franz Joseph *m. p.*

Verlag der Stadt Wien. — Entwurf von R. Lechner (Wilh. Müller), k. u. k. Hof- und Universt.-Buchhandlung. — Biographie von Dr. Leo Smolle. — Druck von Ch. Reisser & M. Werthner, Wien.

a sanatorium. The domestic regime at home then became very strict in order that the dreaded disease might not be passed on to the children. He was in a separate room much of the time, his eating utensils were kept and washed apart and, saddest of all, he could never kiss us, only stroke our heads. In those days I viewed other children's fathers who were healthy with some incredulity and wonderment.

The fact that my parents did not share the same bedroom on account of his tuberculosis must have affected my thinking, for I remember an occasion when the subject under discussion had to do with relationships, and I aired the opinion – a very rare occurrence then for a child to be involved in such talk – that Papa was not really related to me, with the emphasis on 'really'. That did not by any means signify a lack of affection on my part but a difficulty in believing otherwise for want of any physical evidence. I think I bestowed on him the status of a much loved lodger. This caused great mirth and I felt puzzled and mortified.

My sex education, such as it was, was given to me by a succession of maidservants. It must be said that to have had one maid was not then in Vienna a sign of affluence. Life in the country was very hard for peasants and smallholders, and many girls came to the city to seek employment and were found places with families through the medium of convents. In good homes they learned how to cook and sew and housecraft generally, and though their wages were small they managed to save and build up a trousseau from gifts at Christmas. I enjoyed going shopping with my mother when she might buy a pair of sheets, or towels or a tablecloth for just that purpose.

We had one girl, Terese, Resi for short, who was clever and could draw and had the imagination to help us with charades when my cousin Ernestine came to visit. Ernestine was the daughter of my father's sister Emilie, who, with her husband – Uncle Hans to us – had a tailor's business in the elegant spa town of Karlsbad (Karlovivari), then in Czechoslovakia. Ernestine, or Erni, was their only child and went to boarding school in Vienna, since her parents were fully occupied with their work. They came to spend holidays either in their flat in Vienna or took Erni back to Karlsbad.

I knew that Aunt Emilie was Uncle Hans's second wife, he having been widowed and left with a daughter with whom my aunt was said to have a good relationship. The two stepsisters also were close, notwithstanding a considerable difference in age. Cousin Mizzi, on her rare visits to us was greatly admired; blonde and blue-eyed, she took after her father who was not Jewish. Not only her looks, but her voice and manner generally charmed us all.

The shortage of money never seemed to interfere with or curtail the many activities that could be pursued for very little cost: there was walking, swimming and in the winter ice-skating. We watched the thermometer anxiously to see whether the temperature had fallen sufficiently low so that the ice rink, some twenty minutes' walk away, would be sure to be frozen. When the snow came there was tobogganing at a nearby hilly parkland area, a favourite spot for young and not so young alike.

Music lessons, though, cost money and for that reason were erratic over the years; possibly for that reason they were all the more appreciated. Peter and I did eventually attend lessons regularly at a music school, and nearly every Sunday morning we trotted off to orchestra rehearsal, for the director of the school prided himself on running an orchestra which, while having plenty of scope for string players and woodwind, provided scant opportunity for piano beginners. Still, dreams come cheap and I lived eternally in the hope of being allowed to 'accompany' such exciting pieces as the 'Triumphal March' from *Aida* or some stirring excerpt from *Nabucco* or perhaps one or other of the pieces from the usual Viennese Strauss repertoire. In the meantime just attending these rehearsals seemed a privilege and I had to content myself with playing for our own music-making at home. It was such joy to accompany my brother – no doubt atrociously – when he sang some of the old ballads, such as 'The Clock' by Löwe, where the text, whilst speaking of the watch the singer carries on his person, really refers to the heart and the pulse it beats. There were arias from *The Magic Flute*, from *Don Pasquale* and then the Schubertlieder of course, and sometimes we would reverse our roles and he would play for me to sing, one of my favourites being Gounod's 'Ave Maria'. Not till years afterwards would I find out that Gounod had appropriated Bach's *Prelude No. 1 in C Major* from the first book of Preludes and Fugues, the *Wohltemperiertes Klavier*, for the entire accompaniment over which he had written his own melodious singing part.

For the annual concerts in the beautiful hall of the Palais Palffy in the Josefsplatz in the city centre extra 'professional' players were engaged at minimal cost, among them out-of-work musicians or musicians who had seen better days. One of these, looking careworn and emaciated, told of his experiences when he was part of a street playing group during the bad times of unemployment in the Twenties. One of the group had to be on the lookout for policemen, as busking and begging were forbidden, and when he gave the alarm the players had to make a rapid getaway, with instruments hidden away and the piano lifted deftly by many hands and taken out of sight into the nearest courtyard. My favourite musician was a violinist who was often to be seen performing at the tram stop where we would wait for transport. He had a monkey on his shoulder, prettily dressed in a red waistcoat and holding out a tray for alms to the passers-by. The piece that appealed to me was the *Serenata* by Tosselli, which he played with great feeling, or so I thought.

Holidays were wonderful times. During the Easter break we were often invited to Rohatec in Czechoslovakia, where my Uncle Julius and his family lived, and there enjoyed a totally different and freer lifestyle. My uncle, my mother's brother, a tall, gentle man with a loveable and kindly nature, went about his work, moving to and from the chocolate factory only a short distance from the house, with quiet assurance, but always making a little time for us children. Aunt Bertha on the other hand had an exuberant personality which even to us children seemed a splendid foil to that of her calmer husband. Her family had originated in Poland, she spoke a number of languages, was beautiful and, in our eyes, exotic. It was clear that she was her children's friend and that she managed to rule her two daughters, Edith and Marietta, with love rather than authority.

Their house, which was built in the style of a bungalow, was large and commodious with a separate playroom for the children where we could devise our own entertainment, partly with the aid of a gramophone, the kind that boasted an enormous horn, and a selection of records which we were free to use. The garden provided us with ample space for energetic outdoor activities, where we could run about to our hearts' content, play games or take our turn on the swing. On occasions there were outings of which only two stand out in my memory, one to Brno where we saw the castle and the ancient catacombs. I was terrified to see the instruments of torture in the subterranean dungeons. My uncle's chauffeur was our *cicerone* then and it was he also who took us to the River Morava where one could swim and also hire rowing-boats. Peter and the cousins were determined to go out in a boat, but I was more wary and stayed behind. They seemed to be gone an eternity and I was all alone when the adults came to fetch us. What transpired and what later made the headlines in the local paper was that their boat had drifted too far down the river. They went over the weir, the boat capsized of course and they were pulled from the water by some fishermen out in their craft. When they learned that the children were the family of Direktor Pollak they demanded a ransom, which my uncle promptly paid! I daresay had they not asked for it they would have received just as much as a reward.

Thanks to the munificence of Aunt Adele and Uncle Hermann we were also taken on unforgettable holidays in Tyrol, Salzburg and Vorarlberg. During the winter months I know my uncle pored over maps and timetables planning these exciting sojourns which were anticipated with great pleasure and were never disappointing. First, the long train journey heading west from Vienna, then by Postbus (which was a lifeline to the villages, bringing mail and passengers and often picking up loads to be delivered from one village to the next. Coloured bright yellow, like the post boxes in Austria and bearing the insignia of the state post office, it was instantly recognisable as it rocked and rumbled along country roads) to the point where the road ended, and then, on one occasion, by Shanks' pony in the last stage to reach a remote village, following winding paths and stony tracks. The luggage was taken by a mule, that trotted along the way patient and footsure, on ground familiar to him as it was he and his kind who regularly took provisions to the distant villages not yet served by roads.

Walking opened my eyes to nature and brought with it a reverence and awe for the mountains. There was much to see, crossing meadows, following crystal-clear streams, then climbing steadily until in the distance could be discerned the outline of the chalet where one could seek shelter for the night. The accommodation was primitive enough: we slept in bunks and breakfasted on a glass of milk and a piece of brown bread and honey, prepared by the two buxom country girls who looked after the hut and the two or three cows that were grazing outside, with their bells ringing and clanging away, audible a long way off. Now we were ready for the highlight of the expedition, namely a walk across a glacier and snow field, escorted by local mountain guides for whom such work was a means of earning money in the summer. They spoke their own dialect, a mixture of Italian and Tyrolese, which was impossible for us to understand. This secrecy heightened the mystique and a perception of possible danger. Roped together, we negotiated the glacier, partially covered by snow, and never came to any harm, as our Tyrolese friends evidently knew every inch of the terrain.

Back in Vienna after such exhilarating experiences my life once again revolved round school and the everyday activities of our home, and shopping at the grocer's in our street because food was bought fresh every day which without the aid of refrigeration (we just had a simple so-called icebox) was of course essential. For other errands we went a little further, to the Währingerstrasse – such a busy street, with shops and trade of every kind, where the background noise was the whine and jingling of the trams and the clip-clop of horse-drawn carts. There was a seed merchant's business with sacks of different grain displayed on the pavement outside, and very often carters would be there with their horses, taking or making deliveries. The horses were *Pinzgauers*, enormous drays, animals with huge, powerful limbs. They whiled away the time feeding from, and occasionally snorting into, their nosebags, scattering grain in all directions, while they pawed the cobbles, never keeping still for one moment. I can remember now the smell of the oats and how I edged away carefully from these large creatures when I had to pass them on the pavement.

Back also to music lessons – when there were any – and books, which were among my greatest joys and the most welcome presents for birthdays and Christmas. I escaped from what was sometimes a sad home by means of *Wunderbare Reisen* by Selma Lagerlöf, a fictitious account of a tiny boy who flies on the back of a wild goose across Northern Europe and tells of his travels in fascinating and graphic detail. There was the enchanting tale of *Bibi* by Karin Michaelis, the story of the eponymous little Danish girl who walks the length and breadth of her country with sketchbook and pencil, drawing in simple outlines farmsteads, grand castles, churches and other places which formed the illustrations to this book.

The only two visits to the cinema during the years of my childhood still stand out, albeit only as vague impressions: one, *Der Geigenmacher von Cremona* (The Violinmaker of Cremona), dealing with the life and magical environment of the maker of Stradivarius violins, the other *Berge in Flammen* (Mountains in Flames), with Luis Trenker, then a noted actor, in the principal role of a skier who performed feats of great bravery in wartime, presumably the First World War, on the Italian front, in the region of the Trento-Adige, then Austria, now part of Italy. The reason for this war seemed totally incomprehensible to me, and no one explained it, or else I did not ask any questions, but the spectacle was magnificent.

Once I was allowed to join my brother and two friends to go to the Opera, that is the Volksoper, not the Staatsoper, where pupils with their school identity cards could always obtain tickets at preferential prices. We heard *The Barber of Seville* by Rossini and I was entranced. My ambition dating from that time was to become a singer, but it was not to be.

My mother, in addition to running the home and looking after Grandmother, often helped my uncle in his business of *Häuserverwaltung*, a kind of estate agency, mainly concerned with the administration of property on behalf of owners, collecting rents, ensuring the proper maintenance of the buildings for which the agent was legally responsible, and dealing with artisans and contractors engaged on such business. In order to pursue work of this nature one had to be licensed by the authorities, and in order to be licensed one had to pass rigorous examinations which had to do with statutory regulations and the minutiae these entailed as applied to buildings and properties generally and enforced by the municipality. It was thought that Mother would eventually join my uncle in partnership and with that objective in view she embarked on her studies, working all possible and impossible hours, and at the end passing her examinations with flying colours.

All the while though, even as children, we sensed the unrest and threat already making itself felt: the adults spoke of demonstrations, of revolutionary acts, of crises, of the menace of Hitler and the burgeoning of Nazism. There was talk round the dinner table of these strange happenings, but we experienced the danger more realistically when we heard gunfire – it must have been in '34 – at the time of the General Strike, and Peter and I made believe that we had to take cover and crept under the dining table. Although we did not understand the causes of the conflict, we were well acquainted with the names of the paramilitary groups involved in the struggle, the 'Heimwehr' and the 'Schutzbund'; the assassination of Chancellor Dollfuss sent a tremor through the country and certainly affected us children also; the word 'Nazi' became established in our minds as a very terrible epithet. We knew that some of our fellow pupils at school already belonged to the outlawed Nazi youth party, not to mention some of the teachers, who had similar sympathies and affiliations, and as a Jewish child I began to sense some misgivings as to who was friend and who was foe, though I must say that I personally never encountered any positive hostility. We were made at that time at school to wear badges with the red-white-red colours of the Austrian Republic and emblazoned on them was the motto '*Seid Einig*'; be united. I only realised much later that in this way the authorities were aping, and trying to compete with, the German Nazis who made the wearing of the hated swastika compulsory for all.

Then in February '37 came my father's death, for me unexpected despite the long illness and the many attempts which were made to find ways and means for a cure. At the time of his death he was away in hospital and my brother and I had not been allowed to visit him, again, so we were given to understand, to avoid being infected by the TB germs. My mother was inconsolable and all the family's attention centred on her; the children's grief, as with many other childish emotions and fears, were not addressed. It was from that time onwards that I learned to deal with joys and sorrows without recourse to friends or family, and to keep the core of my feelings tightly shut away from the gaze of outsiders and therefore, inevitably, often hidden from myself.

In those days mourning was observed for a year and for the first few months even I as a child wore much black and a black armband to signal to the world one's loss. This caused me no end of embarrassment as I did not know how to deal with kindly enquiries and comments. However, youthful resilience overcomes bereavement, the months passed and early in January '38 when I came home from school saying that we had been asked who would like to go on a week's skiing holiday Mother thought it would be very good for me, and after lengthy family consultations it was decided that I should put my name down for it. My Uncle and Aunt would help with the cost and my cousin Erni would give me her old anorak, but I was to have new trousers and a beautiful red and white striped scarf – all in all, happiness!

The week in the snow in Styria was exciting and the novelty of the sport, the sheer hard work of the daily long walks up the mountainside – there were no ski-lifts – carrying the skis, and an orange in one's pocket to quench the thirst, all this certainly had the effect of clearing my mind of the recent sadness. It was while returning to Vienna, at the junction where all the different ski trains bringing young people back to the capital converged, that I was sharply brought back to reality. From all the corners of the station, like an antiphon of hate, came the chanting and shouting in unison of Nazi slogans, including the ones vowing death to Jews. These were clearly the voices of the as yet illegal Nazi party youth members who now had not much longer to wait for the fulfilment of their dreams, or what they had been brainwashed to believe were their dreams, that of belonging to Hitler's Third Reich. I sat back quietly for the last lap of the journey, troubled and thoughtful, and when I arrived home said nothing of what had occurred.

For me this was indeed the prelude of what was to come so soon, for after the past months, which had been punctuated by political demonstrations up and down the country, came finally the fateful days of March '38 and on the 12th of that month the entry on Austrian soil of German troops. Peter and I were out walking when we heard and saw overhead a squadron of aeroplanes, and we knew instinctively that our lives would never be the same. The proclamation of the annexation by Germany of Austria on 13th March meant for us that our childhood had irrevocably come to an end.

My grandparents with their young daughters.

My young parents in the country with Adele and Julius.

Grandmother's sister, Tante Minna.

Holidays when very young.

My mother with Peter and myself as a baby, c. 1926.

Aunt Bertha with baby Marietta.

A young Julius.

Uncle 'Julo' and my father in the garden at Rohatec with
Marietta and myself.

Holidays in the mountains.

Holidays in the mountains.

Family in the garden with grandmother in Hütteldorf.

My mother at the time of emigration, 1938.

Aunt Adele and Uncle Hermann at home in Hütteldorf.

Peter aged 17.

Chapter Two
Occupied Austria

The changes now happened in rapid succession: anti-Jewish racial laws were proclaimed daily, such as laws of expropriation and directions to expel Jewish pupils from schools. Once I knew that my days at the *Realgymnasium* were numbered, I gave my *Stammbuch* to some of my classmates for their inscriptions and signatures. The Stammbuch was a kind of autograph book and I treasured mine. It was bound in soft brown leather, with gold leaf decoration, and members of the family had already written lines from poetry or of their own devising, some of a didactic character, some in a moralistic vein, but to me always significant. My dear father had made up his own little poem for me, accompanied by a nicely drawn clover leaf whose four petals represented our small family, others had put verses from Goethe and Schiller, or lesser luminaries, and when one of my non-Jewish friends, Herta B., returned the book with her contribution I read:

> *Heil dem, der Demut lernt*
> *nicht durch Demütigungen;*
> *Der, ohne dasz die Welt ihn zwang,*
> *sich hat bezwungen*

which, roughly translated, means:

> Hail to him who learns humility
> not through humiliations;
> who, without the world's constraint,
> has conquered himself.

I realised it contained a hidden message of support and had evidently been inspired by her parents' anti-Nazi sympathies. How cheering it was in those days to find there were good Austrians, when constantly the slogans of *Sieg Heil!* (Hail Victory), *Juda Verrecke!* (Death to Jews), and the aggressive songs of the Nazi movement spoke only of hate.

It now became plain that Austria was no longer a country where its Jewish citizens had a rightful place. Employees were summarily dismissed, anyone might be persecuted and arrested arbitrarily, and people could be turned out of their homes unceremoniously. The word 'propaganda' for the first time entered my vocabulary as applied to the spreading of hideous, false and highly offensive information about Jews, their customs and religious practices, and even a newspaper entitled *Der Stürmer*, a mouthpiece of the SA stormtroopers and the Nazi party generally, which published such items, accompanied by grotesque drawings and caricatures, with the express purpose of inciting blind hatred. Whilst everything Jewish, or what was perceived to be Jewish, was vilified, conversely everything Teutonic and with the outer characteristics of the newly styled 'Aryan' race was extolled. It was time my plaits – all too Germanic – were cut off and my *dirndl* (peasant style, very popular in Austria) dresses with their pronounced national character were discarded; nor would I wear a dark skirt with a white blouse, the uniform of the girls who belonged to the BDM, the Bund Deutscher Mädchen (the League of German Maidens), the female part of the Nazi Youth Movement.

Among the non-Jewish population, that is the 'Aryan' citizens (according to the Nuremberg race laws those of so-called 'pure' German blood were defined as 'Aryan'), there had been much jubilation in the early days of the *Anschluss*, in the streets and in public places, though doubtless there were those – and there must have been some: the silent minority who were not Nazi sympathisers – stayed at home, out of sight. However, we who were Jewish now felt ever more threatened by the turn of events, and it became manifestly clear that emigration was vital, in the true sense of the word. Firstly, my aged grandmother should go to Czechoslovakia to live with Uncle 'Julo' and his family in the belief that there she might be safe.

Our home had been 'requisitioned' by a local Nazi party member who came to look over the flat, found it to his liking and told us to quit within – I cannot remember exactly – a month or so. Much of the furniture, including the beloved piano, was bought at 'bargain' prices, in other words token amounts, by local people, some of the possessions were packed in trunks and suitcases and some were packed for long-term storage in case we should ever return! It was a time of feverish activity for my mother, for as well as attending to the winding up of our home she had to begin seriously to pursue the possibilities for emigration and with that end in view to obtain all the documents required by the authorities, who were bent on making these efforts cruelly difficult by bureaucratic chicanery of every sort.

It was decreed that in our passports we were to be given an extra name – in the case of females 'Sarah' and in the case of males 'Israel' – and in addition on the outer cover there should be printed a large 'J' to signify what was now called the 'race' of the bearer. The purpose again was to procrastinate the issue of the passports, to humiliate us and make life difficult. In retrospect this particular act appears so palpably crude as to make it ridiculous, but at the time it was no laughing matter.

Central to all these plans of emigration was the biggest question of all, that is which country would grant us asylum. Such words as 'visa' and 'affidavit' became household words and synonymous with freedom and deliverance. It was not long before my mother had made up her mind that the country of her choice, if at all possible, would be England. She had read Byron and Shakespeare when she was young and had a fair knowledge of history and the reputation England had for liberalism, and so with single-minded determination she set about the formidable task of obtaining an entry visa. At that time the only way those without specialised scientific qualifications could hope to gain admission was by procuring jobs as domestic servants. In order to do this *The Times* newspaper was acquired, the 'Situations Vacant' columns were eagerly scanned and applications for positions as housekeepers, cooks or cook-generals (as general factotums were called) were dispatched. The replies were awaited with bated breath, the postman's arrival each day giving rise to intense expectancy and the sight of an English stamp bearing the head of King George VI was exciting beyond belief.

At last, after many disappointments, the wonderful thing happened: an English couple in Surrey wanted to employ Mother and were prepared to go to all the trouble of applying to the Home Office for the necessary permission to be granted. Now started the process of improving her knowledge of English and acquiring some skills in English cookery. A large tome entitled *Modern English Cookery* was purchased and was to serve for many years as the principal culinary reference book. Though she faithfully consulted this source and followed its recipes, the results, which were invariably pronounced to be delicious, had not altogether an English flavour.

The time soon came to leave our home. The furniture was gone, the packing cases removed, only our suitcases stood rather forlornly in the hall, ready for the final exit. We were almost at the point of leaving when the doorbell rang (not a welcome sound in those days when 'Brown Shirts' might come and fetch people away) and on opening the door, there stood the familiar portly figure of our concierge carrying a tray of steaming cups of coffee, her practical way of showing us sympathy and compassion. It was an act of bravery, no doubt about it, for had some malicious passer-by reported her to the local party she would have been in trouble.

Frau Z., who had known us, and my grandparents also for many years, was quite a character. Not only concierge, she also presided over the little dairy on the ground floor where we daily fetched our milk, which was scooped out of a large churn with a metal measure and thence poured into whatever receptacle you brought along. In this shop, apart from a few fresh cakes, there was also to be found an enormous contraption which served as an ironing machine. For a small charge all the household linen and sheets of the neighbourhood were pressed. It was set in motion, probably by electricity, by Frau Z. or her hard-working niece, whereupon it groaned and shuddered and performed its task with unfailing efficacy.

Now came a period of an unsettled existence. For a while, it must have been a couple of weeks or so, my mother, brother and I lived in a cheap boarding-house off the Mariahilferstrasse, a novel experience, and from there to lodgings in another part of the town where a woman who had been married to a Jewish husband felt she could risk taking in Jewish tenants. Then, in the autumn, I was to go to school again. I had been directed to attend the only secondary school (*gymnasium*) permitted to a strictly limited number of Jewish pupils, the Chajes Gymnasium, which had always been a Jewish school. I moved in with Uncle Hermann and Aunt Adele in Hütteldorf, where at that time they were still in their small, lovely, airy flat in a pleasant residential part of the suburb, close to gardens and open country.

For a while I could enjoy their company and even the occasional visits from friends and members of the family and hear of their tribulations and plans for the future. I remember once when a cousin of my mother's, Fritz, came with his non-Jewish wife and little boy, and in the course of the afternoon the little chap, perhaps four years old, began to chatter and call out some of the Nazi slogans he had heard. Beginning with his declamation of '*Ein Volk, ein Reich, ein Führer*' (one people, one empire, one leader), he passed easily and merrily on to the nursery rhyme '*Ein Männlein steht im Walde auf einem Bein*', whereupon his parents, fearful that by some extraordinary circumstance he might be overheard and the linking of the Führer with the little man in the nursery rhyme be construed as encouraging subversion in tiny children, shushed the poor child, who was puzzled why his singing of 'A Little Man Stood in the Forest on One Leg' should give such offence!

That was one of the lighter moments of this time though it was symptomatic of the prevailing climate of fear and suspicion when it became almost second nature to talk in whispers, when discussing matters of importance so as not to be overheard. The word 'denunciation', reminiscent of the French Revolution, entered one's language again, and with it the loss of trust between friends, acquaintances and even members of one family. Young people belonging to the *Hitler Jugend* (the Nazi youth organisations) were encouraged to inform on their parents if they were disloyal to the Nazi party.

The serious business of preparing in earnest for our longed-for emigration was now indefatigably pursued by my mother and by my brother Peter. Like my mother, he too had secured a post as chef in the house of a titled family in Huntingdonshire, and, never even having boiled an egg in the past, now set about learning to cook by attending a crash course for similar hopefuls. His job application, also in response to an advertisement in *The Times*, gave details of his education and latter-day cookery training, and as the advertisement had included laconically 'Aga cooker' (something of a mystery to us), he added for good measure 'I am also an Aga cooker'. We never learned the reaction to this extravagant claim; suffice to say that Peter managed to hold down his job for a few months before, no doubt to the great relief of all concerned, he was found alternative employment.

Nearly everyone who needed to emigrate was at that time busily occupied and preoccupied with learning new skills in order to fit themselves for whatever work might come their way in some distant land, wherever that might ultimately turn out to be. There was a burgeoning of schools and institutions created particularly for holding vocational courses of every sort, attended by those who could still afford the luxury of retraining as carpenters, cooks, plumbers or what-have-you. Doctors might have to become mechanics, lawyers bricklayers; in short the name of the game was versatility, and one required readiness to accept any opportunity that might present itself and to prepare for such an eventuality.

As Peter was already seventeen years old he needed to have a work permit and his own separate visa. He was eligible for a place on a so-called children's transport to England purely to facilitate the journey. These 'Kinder' transports were organised with great determination and success by the Jewish community, who disseminated information on how to seek asylum by working in conjunction with Jewish groups and also with Quakers abroad. They did sterling work under most difficult conditions, rescuing children by securing places for them abroad.

With every passing day there was a greater feeling of urgency about our situation. Alarming stories were circulating, of people being 'picked up' and not heard of again, of beatings in police stations and of concentration camps. A woman who lived near us was visited by two SA storm troopers who presented her with an urn said to contain the ashes of her husband, who had been arrested and had vanished. My uncle still staunchly maintained his stance of the patriotic Austrian and at that time firmly believed that Hitler was an upstart who would not last long, and that these were revolutionary days and terrible things happened in all revolutions.

His philosophical outlook, however, was soon to be dented. On 10th November, '38, I was on my way to school – it was a long tram ride across town – when I saw people reading the newspapers with headlines about the assassination in Paris of a German consul by a Polish Jew. It was a gloomy morning and I had some foreboding of danger. I arrived at school and lessons began in an atmosphere of apprehension. It must have been soon after ten o'clock that the headmaster came round to each classroom to tell us to make our way home in small groups as quietly and unobtrusively as possible, for he had received intelligence that arrests were being made and that the school might also be targeted. Four of us decided to try and reach a taxi rank not very far from the school because our homes were a long way off and public transport in these circumstances was out of the question. We told our teacher what we proposed doing and he asked us to take a message to his wife, who would be very worried. He, of course, had to stay behind.

Off we went and succeeded in finding a cab with a woman driver who took us in turn to our homes. When two of us went up the stairs to ring the bell at our teacher's door we could get no reply and we were very troubled indeed at not being able to carry out the errand he had entrusted to us. My home was the furthest away so I was the last to be dropped off. The woman driver asked to leave me at the bottom of the road – she must have known only too well who we were and why we had to return home clandestinely – and I had to explain that I must get some more money from my mother in order to pay her the full amount. I hurried home to find both my mother and aunt in great distress: my uncle had not returned home from an errand and my brother too had disappeared. Before I could make time to hear more I secured the remaining fare and ran down the road, only to find the taxi gone.

What followed on that day remains indelibly imprinted in my memory. How to find out what had happened to the two men? It was a task as daunting as it was puzzling. We left the flat intent on the search, which took us to police station after police station, where no help was forthcoming. Outside one of these I remember seeing a truck, open at the rear, just starting up the engine and driving away, with me running behind it to try in vain to recognise my uncle or brother among the crowd of men it contained. Dejected, we returned home, and it must have been early evening when the doorbell rang and we had to admit a number of men, not in uniform, but declaring themselves to be from the local party, who informed us that we were to be 'concentrated'. What this term meant we could only guess at, but it transpired that they would take us up the road to another Jewish home and that the flat was to be sealed – we knew not for how long – so it could be searched for any 'subversive' material. My mother and aunt were in a state of confusion and alarm, and it was I who advised that we take bedding as I was doubtful the other family would have sufficient for all our needs! It was already dark when we trooped up the road, carrying our quilts, accompanied by two or three of these fellows and one dog. When I stumbled once with my load one of the men told me to mind the dog, whereupon I said cheekily, "I'm not afraid of the dog", with heavy emphasis on the word 'dog'. As soon as I had spoken these words I thought I was going to get a hefty clout, but not so, as the irony of my remark was lost on the man.

Once installed in the small bungalow, the reluctant and somewhat embarrassed guests of Frau L., a widow, her son and daughter, people in their twenties, there was time to talk before getting ready in their sitting-room which had a pleasant smell of timber – the chalet was almost totally constructed of wood – for a night of troubled sleep. Frau L.'s son took a fairly relaxed view of the happenings; his sister, whom we did not then meet, was a nursing sister in one of Vienna's leading hospitals. We learned much later that she and the young non-Jewish doctor whom she had hoped to marry had committed suicide.

I think it must have been on the following day that my uncle and Peter returned, looking white and drawn and manifestly shaken by what had happened to them. They said little and we asked no questions, though it transpired that they had been abused and knocked about, but that somehow or other my brother's *Schülerlegitimation* (a pupil's identity card which all youngsters had and which enabled them to get transport and other tickets at preferential prices and which was proof that he was under eighteen) helped him not to be detained. How Uncle Hermann had got away was not so clear. Others had fared much worse.

Just then, when we were overjoyed at their safe return, came news that I had been allotted a place on the next 'Kindertransport' to Holland, with full instructions about time and place of assembly for departure. Dramatic news indeed. The problem was how soon, if at all, we would be allowed back into the flat so that my clothes could be marked and packed, and of course the necessary suitcase be retrieved. Luck was on our side once more and within a few days, I don't recall how many, while we were still at the chalet up the road, the official seal was removed from the entrance door to the flat and the keys returned.

What might we find? Would the flat have been ransacked and vandalised? Would things have been stolen, cupboards broken open and documents lie scattered on the floor? Not so. Everything was in order, nothing was missing; only my uncle's revolver and a few rounds of ammunition, relics of the First World War, had been removed. What a great surprise and what a relief! For that Aunt Adele was certain that she had to thank one of the posse who had turned us out, a man she and Uncle knew slightly and with whom my uncle had had some dealings. He must have made it his business to restrain the others from any excess disturbance.

Now would begin the task of getting me ready, of sorting and mending clothes, and deciding what else I might need. I was to have a new coat and a hat, and that was exciting, and I enjoyed very much the trip into town and the trying on of different clothes; such a frivolous activity it seemed in these grave days that it had almost something bizarre about it. On another day my aunt took me to buy mending stuff, wools and threads and tapes, but we had to be circumspect in our choice of suitable shops always, for already many windows had daubed over them notices saying 'JEWS UNWELCOME', or 'JEWS NOT ADMITTED', a chilling reminder of the 'new' climate, but we eventually located one. I chose the biggest reel of white cotton that there was, knowing that it must last a long time into emigration when we could not hope to have much money. This wish to plan ahead economically on my part prompted the assistant to remark that one day I would be a very good *Hausfrau*; she had not realised the full significance of my thinking.

Though I expressed no misgivings whatever about my impending departure, the first of the family to have the opportunity to leave, my uncle, no doubt wishing to reassure me about my destination, extolled the goodness of the Dutch people for whom he had a tremendous regard, basing his opinions on the record of that kindly people who had, after the end of the First World War, taken in many children from Austria and Germany who had suffered hardships and undernourishment. I felt suitably sanguine, all the more so as my mother's permit to come to England was soon expected and the necessary papers for Peter's visa were now also in the course of being processed. My aunt and uncle had plans to go to Czechoslovakia, as before long my aunt would have an entitlement to her retirement pension there, and my uncle's idea was to bide time there until what he considered would be the inevitable and early downfall of Hitler. We were not to know then that Czechoslovakia too would be overrun by Hitler and that all these hopes would come to naught.

Chapter Three

Refuge in Holland

The day arrived, 10th December '38, when I was to leave my native city. Departure was from a suburban station, for us very conveniently Hütteldorf, at midnight. The timing was deliberate so as not to draw the public's attention to the expulsion of children in these strange circumstances. It was dark when we left the house, my mother, aunt and uncle, and Peter, the latter two taking it in turn to carry my luggage. We walked for about half an hour and reached the station to find many others there already, perhaps about a hundred or so children, it might have been more, with adults to bid them farewell. There were hushed conversations, mothers encouraging children to be brave, sensible and well behaved; there were some tears, but it was all very orderly, and eventually the time came to board the train, chartered especially for this exodus by the rescue organisations, and the final embraces and goodbyes. The train pulled out without the customary whistles and we were away.

It must have been then that I was overwhelmed by feelings of sadness and the doubts that began to creep through my mind. Would I ever see any of my family again? I knew that my mother's and Peter's papers for England were soon to come, and that the manifold documents which gave permission for them to leave were now also in order, yet in those days, when nothing could be assumed to be certain or secure from one day to the next, there were indeed grounds for apprehension and fear. The tears began to roll down my face as I cried noiselessly and hopelessly for what in retrospect seemed hours, unaware of the train's jolting movements, the hard slatted seats, or the dark ever-changing shadows of the outside world. I knew none of the other children, and I do not think that we spoke for a very long time, each immersed in his or her own troubled thoughts. Then I noticed in the corner of the compartment a very little girl, possibly no more than five years old, hugging a teddy bear, and I realised I was lucky to be thirteen years old and able to understand things, and I managed to stem the flow of my tears.

Little Bertha was not the youngest; there was also Alex, a mere baby. Suddenly the mere presence of these small, vulnerable tiny children had the effect of bringing the rest of us together, and we were friends at once. We felt clumsy and more than a little awkward trying to soothe the little ones, but at the same time happy – if one can use the word in those circumstances – to feel useful in our endeavour to bring them a little comfort. I don't recall feeling tired or hungry though I have no recollection of eating or drinking on the long journey; we must have slept for short spells only, sitting upright on those hard wooden seats; but I do remember that, before we got to the German–Dutch frontier, I was singled out for a body search, possibly because I was so well dressed in my beautiful new coat. Nothing awful happened, and none of my treasured trinkets, my gold chain with the little guardian angel pendant, my dainty ring with the tiny ruby my father had given me when I was eight, or my charm bracelet that had as one of its hangers a miniature train carriage with the letters 'FiG' enamelled on it, signifying ironically *Fahrt ins Glück*, meaning 'Journey into Happiness'. None of these were taken from me.

I think it must have been the evening of the following day, when we crossed the border into freedom, that some of my companions decided to express their feelings about Nazi Germany by spitting out of the windows; they hoped appropriately on the German side! The mood now gradually began to change as we looked forward to our strange new lives and wondered what was awaiting us in this unknown land of milk and honey. Towards eleven o'clock at night we arrived at The Hague. We tumbled out of the train. The small children were taken to one side, to be cared for separately evidently, and the rest of us were escorted to waiting buses which we boarded, somewhat dazed and bemused by sleeplessness and what would nowadays be described as the trauma of the past two days. It was difficult to keep awake and the street lights were no more than a blur and the noise of the engines a constant reminder of movement and confusion.

When the bus eventually came to a halt, we alighted and went into a building that must have been the public baths, where girls and boys were shepherded into different areas, and to my utter astonishment we now had to undress and get ready to shower. I remember the steam from the hot water which made it difficult to see, and also how I tried in vain to cover myself modestly before and after the shower, as I was rather plump and my towel was very small and I could not make ends meet in a literal sense! What disturbed me particularly was the presence of men. I caught the word 'doctor' but could not fathom then, or indeed now, the reason they should have been there. It was only many years later that the unworthy thought crossed my mind that their interest was not strictly medical, for some of the fourteen to sixteen year olds were well developed and not unattractive.

After this extraordinary episode we once more boarded buses and were taken to our 'camp', which was to be our reception area and home for the next six weeks or so. This was a school building, much like so many redbrick Victorian schools in this country, in Copernicus Straat, with a yard to the front, enclosed by a brick wall to the height of about five foot and topped by iron railings. Without further delay we went up to our dormitories and chose our beds, on to which we sank gratefully in a state of complete exhaustion. Sleep came easily and the night was all too short. We were woken by a tug of the blanket at the foot of the bed by a Dutch nurse or helper and told rather briskly in Dutch to get up and go downstairs. The gist of these few Dutch words was fairly easy to understand, accompanied as they were by certain gestures. Rubbing my eyes and getting out of bed with little enthusiasm, I now noticed to my dismay that my bed was in the middle of the dormitory, with perhaps some ten beds all around, and any hope of privacy gained by turning towards the shelter of a wall to dress was gone. The next shock to the system came when going into the corridor in quest of a place to wash and finding a row of sinks with cold water taps only and – what was much worse – no plugs to fill the basins. That meant that one had to wash under the running tap, with the water getting icy cold; it was after all December, the temperature was very low and there was no heating in the corridor. No matter, we had not come here to be mollycoddled!

Then downstairs and into a large hall with long tables set for a communal breakfast, also a new experience. We were given mugs of tea, without milk, and there was bread and butter, but the butter turned out to be margarine, or rather just a scraping of margarine. We were all a little subdued, and although we had been 'saved' the atmosphere was not exactly joyful. Later on, after we had made our beds (supplied by the Red Cross) and coped with blankets and a sheet, quite different from the feather beds we had been accustomed to, we were issued with navy-blue tracksuits, trousers which resembled present-day jogging pants and tops. For the time being these were to be worn in lieu of our own clothes as we were now 'in quarantine'. No one quite knew what that signified, nor did anyone explain. Suitably clad, we were now allowed out into the school yard to run about or stand somewhat disconsolately in groups, talking and reviewing our 'position'.

The meal at midday was no more interesting than breakfast had been; a type of hotpot that contained in one unappetising mass potatoes, onions, carrots and other unidentifiable vegetables. It had been delivered in a large metal container which we soon dubbed the 'refuse bin', as it was so very like the canisters for rubbish at home in the apartment houses where they were kept in back yards or passages. This midday meal was to reappear daily, augmented and slightly improved on Saturdays – or could it have been Sundays? – by thin slivers of meat. The evening meal was more or less a repetition of breakfast, with now and then the addition of a very small piece of Edam cheese. Clearly we were not going to be spoilt, and we were given to understand that this regime was intended not to cause dissatisfaction or anti-Semitism among the unemployed, who were given the self-same diet in soup kitchens.

The highlight of the day was always the distribution of the post in the morning. Letters from home were eagerly awaited and were received with unimaginable pleasure and joy. Then, however, came the next problem to be confronted. We, too, could write home, but our letters had to be handed in unsealed and we knew that they would be read and censored. Therefore, in order that our people at home might be reassured as to our well-being, nothing must be criticised and nothing written that would in any way adversely reflect on our hosts. I had no wish to be ungrateful or to grumble, yet I knew perfectly well that if I were to give the impression I was happy and well looked after I would be left in Holland while my mother and brother emigrated to England. There was no doubt in my mind that this was a very real possibility, with my uncle so enthusiastic about Dutch philanthropy and his advice to my mother, which I had heard even before leaving Vienna, of not taking me to the uncertainty of her exile in England, but to leave me safely in Holland. It was essential then to give a more realistic account of how things stood, and that meant getting letters sent other than through our camp office.

It was not of course simply because of the rather tough conditions that I wanted to get away, but I felt instinctively that Holland was not going to be a safe haven for long – it was too uncomfortably near to Germany and in the shadow of the Nazi jackboot. There were already air raid practices and worried expressions here and there on people's faces. When we were out in the yard for our daily exercise we were delighted to have contact with Dutch delivery boys who, sitting on their bicycles and consequently with their heads above the brick wall, were able to talk to us through the railings. The Dutch are such superb linguists that we found that even these boys, who must have left school at about fourteen, had quite a good knowledge of German. Before long, perhaps a matter of a few days, I was able to ask one of them to post a letter for me home to Vienna, the first that spoke of my anxieties. Fortunately I had been receiving from home international postal reply coupons, which were exchangeable for stamps with which to frank letters back to the country of issue. Thus I felt it was possible to ask the favour of the lad to whom by and by two or three of these letters were surreptitiously passed through the railings.

To my great relief they had the desired effect on my mother who before long indicated in her letters that she would come for me on her way to England and attempt to get permission from the British Consulate for me to accompany her. Knowing that, if all went well, my stay in Holland would not be too long, I found it much easier to put up with discomfort and being hungry most of the time. I managed to enjoy the novel experience of the companionship of new friends in camp, of the kind of fellowship our situation engendered and of the evenings round an imaginary 'campfire', together with Dutch boy scouts who came to visit us. We learned new songs and had, what were for me, rather grown-up conversations about relationships between boys and girls (these were aeons removed from relationships as they are spoken of today, with sexual connotations) and between those in charge of us and ourselves.

The subject that was of particular interest concerned Palestine, as it was then, and the great Zionist hopes connected with it. My own family had never had Zionist aspirations, feeling itself to be Austrian first and Jewish second; in other words, rightly or wrongly, Jewish Austrians rather than Austrian Jews. However, many of my companions had been brought up quite differently and they fervently hoped to go to Palestine eventually and so fulfil their dreams and the biblical prophecy at the same time.

So the days went by. Letters came and went, and we compared notes among ourselves as to the prospects for emigration of the loved ones we had left behind; who had already had an affidavit enabling them to go to the United States, who a permit for England, who might be able to obtain entry to Australia, and so on. It was a red letter day when I heard from Vienna that Peter had at last received his papers for England. He wrote me a postcard virtually immediately on arrival in January '39, and this was followed soon after by a small packet containing biscuits – my first taste of English biscuits, which he must have bought straight after being given his wages. Dear Peter.

Welcome interruptions to the daily routine were occasional escorted walks through the suburbs of The Hague near where we were in Copernicus Straat, and it was interesting to see those Dutch houses, how the architecture struck us then, the burghers' houses so neat and solid, with their steps invariably scrubbed and the brassware brightly polished. On one of these outings we reached Scheveningen and walked amongst the dunes. It was there that I had my first glimpse of the North Sea, and in the cold grey light of December it looked stormy and threatening. In a sense it was in harmony with our preoccupations and premonitions.

Whilst among ourselves we had talked much of how we felt and of the things that concerned us, I do not recall any dialogue with the adults who looked after us. Looking back I do believe that not one of us felt as if anyone cared about us except the sweet and gentle Red Cross nurse whom we called '*Schwester Puppe*', 'Sister Doll', for she was so pretty and kind to us. We loved her for that and for making us cocoa at midmorning, a practice that ceased when she left, to our great disappointment, to get married. She told us that she and her husband-to-be were going to the Dutch East Indies, as they were then, at that time still a Dutch colony. To each of us who had asked for it she gave a small photograph of herself which I have kept all these years. I pray that she never fell into Japanese hands during the subsequent war when so many valiant Dutch people were captured and suffered horrendously.

Our time in Copernicus Straat was coming to an end, and our new home was to be a country house outside The Hague, called

Overvoorde. The boys and the younger children were to go elsewhere and we, the thirteen to sixteen year olds, were taken to the house, standing in its own grounds a few miles out of town, which was to be my home until I left the country. The environment was pleasant and we were allowed to roam within the boundaries of the park-like garden, which was surrounded by ditches and hedgerows. Inside there were rooms that were quite homely and vastly more agreeable than the bare schoolrooms of our previous dwelling. We were five or six to a bedroom and – best of all – there were now bathrooms where we could take hot showers. Two tall women were in charge, one was called the 'director', the other, in nurse's uniform, 'sister'. The sister was severe looking and neither lady was very approachable. There was not much love lost between us. Our food was still brought in the familiar containers and we had almost become accustomed to it. The two ladies' food came separately and contained finer fare. As two of us were always, in rota, given the task of serving the ladies their meals, clearing and washing up afterwards, we knew what their menus were. I am still a little ashamed, thinking back, that when it fell to me to do duty as waitress and washer-up, I scooped up with my fingers out of the dustbin some left-over milk pudding that had been thrown away and ate a few mouthfuls with great relish.

There were weekly visits from members of the 'committee' who had been involved in the organisation and carrying out of the rescue plan which had brought us to Holland. One of these ladies, the wife of a judge, invited a group of us to her house to tea; dainty, small cakes were passed round, and we were keen to show our good manners by taking only one when in fact we would have liked to polish off the lot. It was a beautiful, comfortable home, but we felt awkward and ill at ease, though our hosts were kind and for once we were spoken to individually and with understanding. There is no doubt though that the 'refugee' mentality was becoming established, and with it a gulf which divided us from those more fortunate than ourselves who belonged to, and were part of, their own society.

A delightful outing which has remained fixed in my memory was when we were taken in buses to a cinema in The Hague to see a Deanna Durbin film, a musical called in Dutch *Wildzang*, for us adolescents the most wonderful escapist entertainment. I found it entrancing and was transported into another world and we all sang the songs we remembered on the way back to Overvoorde and in the days that followed, and they served to relieve the monotony of our routine.

At that time there were still no lessons of any sort, though there was some talk of school in the near future. Apart from the daily chores, including doing the laundry, when I found it quite difficult to lift and wring out sheets by hand, using old-fashioned copper boilers and large, heavy galvanised zinc basins, we were left to our own devices quite a lot. It is still a mystery to me how we did pass the days without what is nowadays taken for granted, namely television, radio, recorded music and so on and so forth. Yet I am sure that we were kept busy, doing housework, writing letters, mending our clothes and cleaning our shoes, going for walks, and no doubt talking endlessly about plans for the future.

When one of the girls was ill I hit upon the idea of a 'treat' for her and with a friend decided to make our way to the nearest shop to buy a bar of chocolate. In order to do this we would have to get out of the grounds by stealth as it was absolutely forbidden, and go along the main road some distance, we knew not quite how far. The adventure worked well: we were not observed scrambling through the hedge at the perimeter of the park, and then we walked, perhaps a mile or two, before reaching houses and what seemed like a post office cum village stores. Now the next obstacle had to be overcome, that is the lack of money. I had brought some of my postal reply coupons in the hope of trading these in for cash though, strictly speaking, they were not negotiable. I think the kindly assistant guessed our plight and gave us two bars of chocolate, the first we had seen since coming to Holland, in exchange for the postal coupons. Mission accomplished! We returned triumphant and slipped through the undergrowth, having been away no more than one and a half hours, during which our absence had not been noticed. The chocolate, even if it did not bring about a sudden recovery, was a wonderful morale booster for the patient.

At last the longed-for day came when my mother arrived and I was taken to the station in The Hague to meet her. She alighted from the train and I saw her come towards me, dressed predominantly in black, and after a quiet embrace we were taken back to Overvoorde, together with her luggage, and I explained that she would be able to stay at the home for two nights before the departure to England. My friends Meta, Lilly and Hannerl were happy to meet my mother, the first parent to be able to come to Holland to claim a child and – God willing – take her to the destined place of emigration. It was an event not only in my life but in their routine also and raised the hopes that one day they too might be reunited with their loved ones.

On the following day outside the gates of Overvoorde we boarded the bus which would take us into town for the appointment at the British Consulate where my future was to be decided. We saw an official to whom my mother explained the situation, how she wanted to take her daughter with her to England in order to keep her small family together, my brother having already gone to England separately. Without any fuss, and with a minimum of delay or prevarication, the answer was yes and an entry was made in my mother's passport that would satisfy the immigration authorities in Harwich as to my legal right to enter the country. After all the agonising over the likelihood of this permission it seemed all too easy. We thanked our interlocutor and left the building in high spirits. The Hague seemed the most beautiful place on earth, every person we saw in the street had an aura of saintliness in my eyes and I seemed to be treading on air.

Before returning to Overvoorde I asked mother whether we could possibly buy some oranges to take back to the girls for a celebration. It was asking quite a lot of her because all she possessed – that is, the full allowance granted to Jews in emigration by the Nazi authorities – was the grand sum of ten German marks, which had to last us until she got her first monthly wages in England. Nonetheless oranges were purchased and there was great rejoicing when we returned and my friends learned the news. Now the matter of the fare to England was the next hurdle to overcome. Frau von H., one of the committee ladies, agreed to lend Mother the necessary amount and Mother promised to repay it out of her wages in small instalments. This is what she actually did, but after three or four months the kind woman wrote to say that she did not wish Mother to continue paying.

It seemed as if the gods had been on my side. Had it not been so my life would have gone very differently. My immediate friends, Meta, Lilly and Hannerl did survive the subsequent invasion of Holland, though Hannerl suffered much in a concentration camp. Meta worked with the French Resistance, which she reached by circuitous routes, having been passed off to begin with as a Dutch agricultural worker, but ended up after harrowing wartime experiences in Israel, as did also Lilly. Many of the others perished.

At eleven o'clock at night, two days after Mother's arrival, days which had been crowded with activities and emotions, we sailed for England from Hoek van Holland. The two boy scouts who had become friends of mine cycled all the way from The Hague to say goodbye, but not surprisingly never found me. Sadly I never saw them again and it was not till after the war that I learned from my friend Meta of their fate: one of them, Herbert, perished in the Holocaust whilst his friend Hans managed eventually to reach Israel.

Chapter Four

England!

The crossing was uneventful but it was stormy and, unaccustomed as I was to travel by sea, I was very sick. Whilst I used the washbasin for the purpose, having been taken ill very suddenly, a stewardess pounced on me, saying, "You can't be sick in here!" and though my English was very inadequate I longed to reply, 'Oh yes, I can!', but of course refrained, and instead accepted the proffered brown paper bag, the proper receptacle for such an emergency. We arrived in Harwich looking green and hollow-eyed, but exultant to be on English soil. Then we boarded the unfamiliar looking train, with its separate compartments, upholstered comfortable seats, so unlike the ones I had sat on when leaving Vienna. We settled with great relief for the short journey that took us through grey and barely discernible countryside in the dim, early morning light to London, Liverpool Street Station. From there we went by taxi to the employment agency which had dealt with Mother's job on behalf of her employers. I am not sure of the reason for this visit, but believe it was in order to obtain a small advance on the first month's wages so as to be able to pay the fare to Surrey, our ultimate destination, the ten marks having by then been exhausted. There we had quite a friendly reception and were soon on our way to Victoria Station to embark on the final lap of the journey.

We arrived in Surrey and were met by the family's chauffeur who, I do believe, was astonished and perhaps a little disappointed to see us, well dressed and with ample luggage, so unlike the vision he had probably harboured of 'refugees', more picturesque, with head scarves and bundles of clothing carried on their shoulders! We in turn were very impressed with Mr B.'s smart appearance in his uniform and peaked cap, and with impeccable manners he opened the car doors for us, stowed away the cases and took us to the lovely house, set in the pretty Surrey countryside, which was to be Mother's place of work.

My father in World War I uniform.

Peter in Airborne Division uniform.

Cousin Ernestine with her step sister Mizzi and parents on
holiday in Italy.

Myself aged 3.

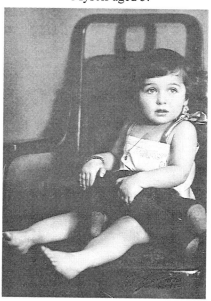

Cousin Edith aged approximately 16.

Cousin Marietta with her English adoptive mother and
brothers, August 1939.

Cousin Marietta aged 13.

Sister 'Puppe', Yoopee de Haas.

'Overvoorde'.

At Scheveningen.

Joyful reception of the cake.

From :

WAR ORGANISATION OF THE BRITISH RED CROSS
AND ORDER OF ST. JOHN

To :

Comité International
de la Croix Rouge
Genève

Foreign Relations
Department.

Expéditeur   SENDER   Absender

Name ...... Miss Leicht

Nom
Christian name .... Lisbeth
Vorname Prènom
Address ......
Adresse

MESSAGE   Mitteilung

(Not more than 25 words)   (25 mots au maximum)   (Nicht über 25 Worte)

Meine Liebsten,hoffen Ihr seid wohlauf,lange
ohne Nachricht.Arbeit erfolgreich,studiere.
weiter. Uns dreien geht es gut,hoffen auf
baldiges Wiedersehen.
.... Küsse Mama,Lisl

Date Datum...... 19/8/43.

Destinataire   ADDRESSEE   Empfänger

Name .. Frau Barcs Tiborné
Nom
Christian name .... - -
Vorname Prènom
Address .... Klotild Utca 22.
Adresse
.... Budapest
.... Hungary

Reply overleaf (not more than 25 words)
Réponse au verso (25 mots au maximum)
Antwort umseitig (nicht über 25 Worte)

1 4 SEPT. 1943

ENVO: 254/282

NACHRICHT MACHTE UNS GLUECKLICH.
AUCH WIR ERHOFFEN BALDIGSTES WIEDERSEHEN.
BLEIBT NUR GESUND. PETER UNSERE GROESSTE SORGE.
GRATULIEREN LISERL. WIR UND JULOS GESUND
SEHNSUECHTIG DIE EUREN.

4 DEC. 1943

Mrs D. received us warmly and without much ado we were taken to our, or rather Mother's, room which I was to share for the time being until other arrangements could be made for me. This room was in the servants' part of the house, separated from the rest by a long corridor with beautiful, old oak floors, glossy with years of polish. It was sparsely furnished, with two iron bedsteads, a washstand, chest of drawers and a narrow wardrobe. Its redeeming feature was the delightful and quite new to us fragrance of a large bar of glycerin soap which seemed to permeate the entire area and remains with me to this day, as also the drift of scent from roses in the rooms downstairs: my first impression of an English house.

The moment of truth had arrived inasmuch as we were now definitely reduced to the status of servants, and though we were so happy to be in England I could not help but feel a pang of resentment on behalf of my mother, so cultured and well-read. Now she would need to make use of her other resources, and with her skills and competence, coupled with great strength of character, adjust to this new life and the humility it called for.

My mother had no more than a few hours to settle into our unaccustomed quarters before taking up her domestic duties, dressed in the neat white cotton overalls bought in Vienna especially for this, her new role as housekeeper. The elegant black afternoon dress made by our old dressmaker at home, who had sewn so many of our clothes and which my aunt and uncle had fondly imagined she would be wearing, spending part of the afternoons in the company of our hosts, hung unused in the wardrobe, for there was no social intercourse between Mr and Mrs D. and ourselves. Clearly a great gulf divided us, and our status as servants, regardless of what we had been in the past, would separate us according to the dictates of class which then prevailed.

At this particular time there were no other servants in the house as two girls had had to return to Wales to their home for health reasons, so we were told. One of them had had a very nervous disposition and possibly the prospect of foreigners invading what they considered their terrain was a little too much for them! Mother started her day, consequently, before six o'clock in the morning, doing all kinds of cleaning jobs before preparing a beautiful cooked breakfast served on shining silver entrée dishes in the lovely old dining room, furnished in exquisite country house taste complete with antiques. Later, the menu for the rest of the day was decided by the lady of the house when she visited the kitchen and with pencil and paper at the ready gave her instructions, coupled with certain explanations of terms and terminology regarding English food as yet not understood by the 'foreign' housekeeper. At one time Mother was nonplussed by Mrs D. asking specifically that the custard was not to be made with 'Bird's', and mother couldn't quite make out how the winged creatures were involved, not being familiar with the brand name of the powder used instead of fresh eggs for the making of custard. All things considered, Mother managed beautifully. Her intelligence and her competence, not to mention her readiness to work from morning till night, saw her through, and as for me, I was honorary scullery maid, dealing with piles of washing up in the antediluvian back-kitchen with its primitive sink and a wooden draining board, which became at certain times of the day and evening my own familiar habitat.

Not long after we had arrived at Ham House, on one of Mother's free afternoons, I asked her to bake a cake for the girls back in Holland and I helped her with its preparation. As soon as it had cooled it was carefully packed and dispatched, and before long we had a letter back and enclosed in it was a snapshot that testified to its safe arrival and enthusiastic reception.

With other members of the staff at Ham House Mother had good relations. The chauffeur's wife would ask us to Sunday tea, when she brought out her best china and gave us dainty sandwiches, or bread and butter and jam, served emulating the style of the 'master and mistress', as the employers were mostly referred to. They were good people, and their standard of manners and behaviour generally would do credit today to folk in much more exalted positions. They had a little boy, an only child, whom I sometimes helped with his piano practice.

The gardener, who put in an appearance regularly to bring the daily supply of produce, was more of a rough diamond. A big man, he came to the back door looking rather dishevelled and with his mop of unruly hair in need of brush and comb, and handed over the vegetables dug freshly from the garden. He liked to dally a while to talk to the new housekeeper. She, however, was impervious to his rugged charm and was far from encouraging, listening only perfunctorily and not for long to his tale about his wife who was forever 'poorly' and whom, in fact, we never did see.

I knew, however, that before long certain decisions about my future would have to be taken as, to begin with, I was to stay with Mother only temporarily, that is until such time as the Jewish committee in London was able to find a home for me with an English family. It was possibly a week or two after our arrival at Ham House that we made the journey to London, to Bloomsbury House, to join a throng of other refugees on similar quests. There were so very many people there, with problems as numerous as their numbers, and we saw clearly the enormity of the difficulties which seemed almost to overwhelm the hard-working helpers. The few hours of waiting we spent there amongst this human conglomerate of displaced persons were disheartening and depressing, and then Mother decided we would wait no more, we would return to Surrey and she would ask Mrs D. whether I might be allowed to stay with her. I am not sure if I was glad or not about this change of direction, as I felt I would be tolerated rather than welcomed, and that therefore my position would be somewhat ambivalent.

Whatever my feelings, these were soon put aside as the plan for my future began to take shape: I was to go to school again - hurrah! - and after these past months without any formal or informal lessons the prospect was exciting; even more so after I had been taken to the County School for Girls in R. in Surrey for a preliminary interview and I saw what to me was a fine, redbrick building, set amid lawns and shrubberies, and with tennis courts at the rear. Soon came my first school day. From the village halt at N. I caught a train to the bigger town where I changed to a bus which took me right up to the school gates. I had no school uniform as yet and felt like a bird of paradise in my Viennese coloured jumper and skirt and longed for the day when I could merge into the general scene and look like an English schoolgirl.

I was taken into my classroom by the form mistress, one Miss S., who introduced me, told the girls where I had come from and asked them in no uncertain manner, against a background of suppressed giggles, to teach me good English only. They must have taken this admonishment to heart, for in all the time I was there I never heard slovenly speech, let alone swear words. Without exception my classmates were kind to me, and although a great deal was strange I soon settled into the orderly routine of the school, enjoying the vastly more personal relationship which existed between staff and pupils, who were called by their first names, in contrast to the practice in Austria where we had been addressed by our surnames.

The regime was so different altogether, what with school hours from 9 a.m. to 3.45 p.m., compared with the 8–1 timetable at home, the lunches at school, so quiet and well-mannered, so much so that to begin with I felt quite ill at ease, holding my knife and fork in continental fashion which I thought might be taken for bad manners, and gradually struggling to eat like the others, balancing food on the back of forks, rather precariously it seemed to me. The tables in the refectory were arranged in such a way that there were about eight girls to each one. The food was brought in from the kitchen on trolleys by helpers in uniform, the neat striped dresses, and caps to match, of maidservants, and for each table there were separate dishes containing meat, vegetables and so on from which the monitresses served the rest of us. Everyone having been given her plate, the monitress then said grace before the meal could begin. It took me a little while to catch hold of what 'For what we are about to receive may the Lord make us truly thankful' was all about because the words were so rapidly spoken that they were indistinguishable from one another; it was followed by an injunction to 'start ahead' and we set to, never speaking except to ask for the salt and pepper to be passed. I did feel extremely lucky to be in such civilised, albeit unaccustomed, company and did not find it at all irksome to have to conform to this new set of rules. I had a lot to be thankful for, knowing that my mother had to pay three guineas a term for my school fees ('guineas' was the refined term for the sum of £1 and 1 shilling), a not inconsiderable amount out of her monthly wages of £5.

As regards the actual lessons, these were pleasurable, even though in history and geography I didn't do so well because the syllabus was so very different from the previous Austrian one. Chemistry proved downright impossible. The girls had done one year in the subject, whereas I in Vienna had done one year in physics. When faced with a test paper quite early on it might have been Chinese for all it meant to me, and I had no alternative but to hand in a blank sheet when the papers were collected. Miss B. expressed disapproval with the words 'You haven't even tried' and I felt humiliated for once, and once only at R.

Languages, however, were a different matter; the only difficulty there was my pronunciation of Latin which led my teacher to believe that I got it all wrong, until fortunately my written work proved otherwise. The English lessons presided over by my form mistress, Miss S., were my favourite ones, and I soon felt I was beginning to make progress.

Assembly in the mornings always took place in the large school hall in the presence of the headmistress, Miss A., a frail white-haired lady, who suffered cruelly from rheumatism. There were hymns which I liked very much and in which I joined, though I did not know them, and managed to do so by keeping roughly a quarter beat behind the others. When prayers were said I cast my eye surreptitiously round to observe the teachers who were lined up at right angles to ourselves, their backs to the wall, with their eyes closed in concentrated worship. That impressed me a lot. It troubled me, however, to take part in what was obviously a Christian service, and one day I plucked up courage to ask one of the mistresses about it. She reassured me that it was perfectly in order for me to participate as the main part of the service was the reading of Scripture and that, she said, was after all our common heritage. I needed to know no more and henceforth enjoyed being introduced to the richness of the English hymnal.

During the lunch break I would often write long letters to my beloved aunt and uncle who were still in Vienna and then post them on the way home. On one occasion, not having managed to finish a letter at school, I did so while waiting for my train at R. station and then ran down the stairs from that particular platform to a lower level where the letterbox was to be found. Hurriedly I returned to what I thought was the correct point of departure, but, never having been blessed with a good sense of direction, I mistook the train I saw already waiting to leave for mine, got on it, and to my great dismay presently found it was going towards London, the opposite direction to where I wanted to go. Not only that, but I had also boarded a first-class compartment where I found myself in the company of two rather forbidding ladies, definitely upper class, who proceeded to question me closely as to my origins. They remarked, among other things, that I looked rather well for a refugee, and that Herr Hitler could not be so bad. I was dumbfounded and, sensing the hostility, totally at a loss for words. It would have taken a considerably greater command of the language than was mine at that time to explain how things stood in Nazi Germany, and, feeling rather crushed, I was relieved to leave the train at the next stop, which was Croydon, where this time I found the correct platform for my return journey. This was the first encounter in England to show me that not everyone was on our side, so to speak, as I had quite naively believed.

Aside from this experience life continued pleasantly and uneventfully. At school I made friends, but never once did I speak of my earlier times either in Austria after the *Anschluss*, or in Holland as a refugee. The treatment and persecution of Jewish people was a particularly taboo subject, as I felt instinctively that even the knowledge of such things might somehow corrupt these young people who, to me at any rate, seemed utterly innocent, totally ignorant of, and removed from, evil. Nor did they ever pry or ask difficult questions; they must have had an innate sense of tact and consideration.

Once or twice I was invited to girls' homes. I felt unable to reciprocate, not having a home I could really call my own, and was partly embarrassed and partly worried lest my English hosts think me and my mother, of course, both ungrateful and inhospitable. An invitation that had to be declined at the outset was one to a garden party. I had read stories in which garden parties were described as delightful social events, typical of English society, with everyone impeccably dressed (and behaved), daintily nibbling wafer-thin sandwiches and making polite and rather jolly conversation. There was no way I could see myself fitting into this exalted company, though I would have liked and been interested to catch a glimpse of those godlike creatures sporting under trees and on terraces and lawns.

We had now moved from our first home in this country to Staplehurst Farm (no longer a farm, but converted into a fine residence), the home of Mrs D.'s newly married son and his bride, where mother was in sole charge of the housekeeping, which comprised every manner of domestic work. I now had a longer walk to the nearest bus stop to go to school, perhaps half an hour or so, which I found agreeable as a space of time entirely my own. On my way home one day – it was quite hot and I was carrying a heavy school satchel – a car pulled up (there was very little traffic along Surrey country lanes then) and the driver asked whether he could give me a lift. This expression was quite new to me and I wondered whether it might be an improper suggestion. I blushed furiously and in great confusion shook my head, stuttered, "No" and the man drove off with a puzzled expression on his face.

On Mother's free afternoons we would enjoy walking along the lanes and marvelled at this serene, peaceful world, so very different from the one we had left behind. There were times when we tended to think people in England were like ostriches, burying their heads in the sand, ignoring the threat of the expansionist Nazi which that had as its refrain *'Denn heute gehört uns Deutschland und Morgen die ganze Welt'* (today Germany belongs to us and tomorrow the whole world). There were other times when we too were lulled into what was to be a short-lived period of relative freedom from anxiety, when we persuaded ourselves that our pessimism was unfounded and due to our situation.

Many things could be enjoyed. An outing to a teashop in R. and my first acquaintance with a confection called 'Battenberg' cakes – so cleverly constructed of pink and yellow squares – a visit to the cinema to see – and hear – *The Mikado* with its wonderful Gilbert and Sullivan score and text. Little did I know then that my son would one day be cellist in the orchestra of English National Opera and that I would then hear this music again in, oh, such different circumstances. Walking was always pleasurable, and in the warm weather we might meet the 'Stop me and Buy one' vendor of ice cream on his bicycle and sometimes, finances permitting, indulge ourselves in that luxury. If, after school, I had a few pennies left over from what I was allowed for bus fares, I might call into Woolworth's, that mecca of bargains, where at the sweets counter one could buy at an affordable price a kind of chocolate crunch, sold loosely, and broken up by the assistant with a pair of pliers which rather resembled those used by a dentist for the extraction of teeth.

All the while letters passed regularly between ourselves and Aunt and Uncle, who were still in Vienna trying to set in motion their emigration to Czechoslovakia where, as had been their hope, they would mark time until the day when Austria and the world were freed of the terror of Nazism. When Chamberlain came back from his notorious visit to Hitler with his message of 'Peace in our Time' we were glad that, as it seemed then, war might be avoided, though we knew in our heart of hearts that a compromise solution was hardly realistic, and that the kind of revolution within Germany which might topple the regime was by now well-nigh impossible, with the power of the Gestapo, the secret state police, and all the inhuman means at their disposal exercised by a ruthless, authoritarian government, silencing any dissent.

No one was left in any doubt, however, about the intentions of the leadership of the Third Reich when, in the summer of '39, Czechoslovakia was also invaded. This was a dreadful blow to us, knowing that my Uncle Julius, my mother's brother, and his family were now also trapped. At that time the last direct communication my mother had had from her brother was dated December '38 (see Figure 1 and 1a). In it he writes

> *Es ist ein bischen schwer ihr das Alles begreiflich zu machen, was natürlich nicht zu verwundern ist, da manchmal auch ein jüngerer Mensch es nicht fassen kann, dass alles das, was sich um einen herum abspielt, Wirklichkeit sein soll...*
>
> It is a little difficult to make her [Grandmother] understand all that is taking place around one, which is not to be wondered at, as even a younger person can hardly conceive it all as reality.

Grandmother, at that time eighty-three, writes her own letter on the reverse side saying she is unhappy not to be able to embrace her loved ones before their departure. She asks for news and enquires separately about me and whether Mother has heard from me in Holland. Towards the end of the letter she writes *'Wie gerne wäre ich jetzt bei Dir, liebe Gertrud, damit Du nicht ganz allein wärst'* – 'How much I would like to be with you now, dear Gertrude, so that you would not be all alone'.

We had thought that Grandmother had found sanctuary in Czechoslovakia and that she might end her days in the loving care of her son, his wife and their daughters. Now it was not to be. Where would they be able to go? What would become of the old lady? Aunt Adele's plans and preparation to find temporary exile in Czechoslovakia would never come to fruition. A new, desperate situation had arisen.

Mother immediately begged her employers, Mr and Mrs D., to apply to the Home Office for permission for them to come to England,

and, to their great credit, but also because they had come to respect and admire my mother's integrity and her capacity to adapt herself to her new life, they did set things in motion, but it was not to be. That summer, in July and August '39, the Home Office did not expedite such applications with the haste we so anxiously wished for. Time was running out, and when war was declared on 3rd September 1939 we sensed with foreboding what it meant for England and for us all.

Chapter Five

War Declared

I remember our headmistress announcing the grim news at school assembly, and a hushed, awesome silence fell over all present. It signalled the end of an era and the beginning of we knew not what. Lessons were resumed and everything had an unaccustomed seriousness about it. As the weeks passed, although it was still 'the phoney war' and 'all was quiet on the western front', precautionary measures were being taken for the time, yet to come, when the country would be subjected to air attacks. Shelters were built and there was regular drill for leaving the building. Before long we had an influx of pupils from London who were being evacuated to the safety of the country. New premises were acquired within the residential area close to the school and we had to have our lessons in various locations.

Young men were now being called up for military service. Peter, who was now almost nineteen, tried very hard to enlist but was turned down because he was a foreigner. At that time, early in the war, there was not yet an opportunity for us to make a contribution to the war effort, much as we wished to do. It was a great shock then when in May '40 Peter, along with countless other 'aliens', was apprehended and taken off to internment. I think he was allowed to write only a brief postcard giving us the scantiest information, from which we gathered that he was being sent to the Isle of Man. The next bombshell fell when I was given a message at school to return home immediately, my mother having telephoned that she too was to be interned, and that we were going to be picked up that same afternoon to be taken away. Naturally I would be going where she was going even though, being under eighteen, I was not myself a candidate for internment. I made my way back home in a daze of bewilderment and disappointment that our lives should yet again be turned upside down. Once home, there was no time for feeling sorry for ourselves or to feel angry, but it was necessary to pack a couple of suitcases with our most essential clothing and personal possessions. We could not help but smile at the idea that anyone like ourselves could be thought to be a threat to the security of the country, but realised these were panic measures as the war, day by day, became a reality, and it was clearly necessary to catch spies. We presumed that the easiest and fastest method to that end was to haul in the sheep and the goats alike and postpone their segregation until a later date. Furthermore, living as we did on the edge of a small airfield – the property of the family who hosted us – we might, had we been Nazi spies, have done useful work for the enemy.

Curiously, of our journey to the Isle of Man I remember only separate incidents: the ride in the car from Staplehurst Farm to Dorking, and after further travelling – I know not how – being taken to a boxing arena in Liverpool, there to await transfer to the boat that would take us across to the island. We spent one night in the boxing arena, the collecting point for some hundreds of women, some also with their children, and I recall trying to make myself comfortable sleeping across the tip-up seats which were apt to close in on one as soon as one shifted one's position. It was quite funny at times. I think bread was handed out to us the following morning, and mugs of tea also, before we made our way under escort to the docks. There were jeering groups along the jetty who hurled abuse at us, and again we found it ironic and not devoid of black humour to be called 'Bloody Germans', having to endure insult added to injury.

On board ship it became evident that it was vastly overcrowded and we were standing or sitting on the floor and on any available space close together and wondering whether the ship would sink. It didn't, however, and after this uncomfortable crossing of the Irish Sea, we disembarked at Port Douglas whence by a small train we travelled through a very pretty stretch of countryside to Port Erin, our destination and place of confinement for the duration of our internment. Once arrived, we were allocated to the different hotels and boarding houses which had all been requisitioned by the government to accommodate the internees. What an attractive seaside place it was, with a long, curving promenade above the bay, overlooking a wide expanse of sand and rocky outcrops, against a backdrop of hills which we soon learned were beyond the barbed wire perimeter of our camp. 'Our' boarding house bore the propitious name of Strand Cafe, at the lowest end of the sea front and only a few paces away from the shore. It was not as smart as the hotels further up, and I imagine we presented as strange a picture to the landlord and his wife as they did to us. They were Irish, or of Irish extraction, and it soon became clear that their sympathies were more inclined to Nazi Germany than to Britain. To have all their guest houses filled to capacity, courtesy of the British Government, must have been reasonably lucrative for these landlords. They did not have to provide any service as all the work was done by the internees, but it fell to Mrs McC. to dole out the rations of food daily and to deal with one elected representative of the internees regarding any other domestic matters. When one saw the small pile of meat, or vegetables or any other comestibles that would constitute the day's provisions, one was amazed how ingeniously these were transformed into quite acceptable meals. Certainly I was never as hungry there as I had been in Holland, and I was very indignant when I heard some of our fellow internees complain.

Within the little town and along part of the beach we were free to walk, and there were shops to go to, but of course there was no money available to spend, except Mother's small post office savings account which she had so thriftily built up to the grandiose sum of about £30. From that she withdrew negligible amounts for the purchase of wool to enable us to knit. Everyone was knitting; it was virtually the only occupation available in the evenings, with a curfew at nine o'clock, no newspapers allowed, little reading matter and no radio. The garments produced ranged from dowdy shapeless ones to beautifully crafted fashion models. There was much exchanging of ideas regarding patterns and stitches, and I too increased my expertise and sold one of my creations, thus earning enough money to finance a further purchase of wool. My next effort, executed with thin needles and a very close stitch (this meant that one would be engaged on the project for a long time and, hopefully, by its completion one might be released from internment) yielded a fine cardigan, striped in front and plain in the back, with a woven rather than a knitted effect, and it served me for a number of years and was often admired.

It took a little while before the internees organised classes of different kinds, catering for different interests, but regular schooling for youngsters there was not, probably because of the small number of children of my own age. Consequently I opted for a dressmaking course and enjoyed with another girl the walk to Port St Mary where this was being held and run by an attractive young woman who had worked in the fashion trade as a designer and dressmaker. She taught us how to make patterns and drawings, for which my companion showed a wonderful aptitude, but I, alas, none at all. However, I did learn something about the actual making and sewing of clothes which stood me in good stead later in life.

We were a motley crew. There were two German-Jewish women in their thirties with delightful, well-behaved children, my favourites being the very pretty Evie, about six years old, and her brother Herbert, her senior by about three years. Herbert had already a reputation for being a good businessman, which was borne out later in life, being able to save up eleven pennies and then miraculously changing these for a shilling. (This was of course before decimalisation in Britain, when there were twelve pence to a shilling, and twenty shillings to a pound). There was one rather stout lady whose features were not unlike those of Hermann Göring and her rather querulous eleven year-old daughter; there was Mrs L., with whom my mother became quite friendly, whose husband had been in Dachau concentration camp and who spoke fondly of an only daughter in South Africa; a couple of women around forty about whom there was a certain amount of whispering as they were thought to have run a 'disorderly' house. I did know this designation meant something other than just untidiness, but was a little vague as to the full extent of its significance; there were two German women roughly in their thirties whom we suspected of being, if not actually spies, then certainly Nazi sympathisers; there were also two young girls of Austro-Hungarian origin, one of whom had theatrical leanings. Many others have over the years faded from my memory, although even after such a lapse of time I can still see before my eyes the face of the young woman who was expecting a baby and eventually gave birth to it in the hospital at Douglas. A meeting had been arranged for her with her husband while he too was an internee also on the Isle of Man, which must have been highly emotional, but she was released and left for the mainland long before us. Also not forgotten is the picture of the quiet woman with her two pale, fair daughters, who did not seem to mix much with the rest. They were orthodox Jewish and quite possibly deemed us all beyond the pale. Her *bona fide* status, one would have thought, must surely have been impeccable and she should never have come in the first place.

The word 'release' was ever on our lips and those who gradually were able to leave were congratulated and the objects of some envy. When some left, the others set about with renewed vigour to try and have their cases reviewed by approaching the camp authorities and writing to friends in England to intercede on their behalf. As newspapers were not accessible to internees, our knowledge of the momentous events in the outside world were limited partly to rumour, partly to what could be gleaned by listening surreptitiously at the kitchen door of our landlord when the nine o'clock news from the BBC was broadcast. We did know that the war was in a perilous state and that our position could after all not be of burning importance to the powers that be.

All letters, outgoing as well as incoming, were censored, understandably, and of Peter we heard little, save that he had been on the Isle of Man, but we found out that all the men were being shipped overseas. We heard, I know not exactly how, of the sinking of the *Arandora Star* on her transatlantic voyage to Canada with German and Italian prisoners of war as well as Jewish refugees, and thereafter of a further transport to Australia on the *Dunera*. Peter in fact was on the latter and it was a long time before we knew he was safe in Australia. Eventually his renewed attempt to volunteer for the British army was successful, and along with many others he returned and had much to tell. The *Dunera* had been pretty much a hellish ship, the treatment of the internees shameful, and when he told us of being robbed of all his personal possessions and having to exercise barefoot on the deck over broken glass for the entertainment of the guards, we could scarcely believe our ears.

Among the welcome mail was a letter from my form mistress in R. who wanted me to return to school, and in order to do so offered me a place in her house. My heart leapt at the thought, but I found my mother not receptive to the suggestion, and we had no discussion, let alone dispute, on the subject, for I felt instinctively that, were I to go, she would feel this meant the end of the last vestiges of the family, such as it was, with everyone already scattered to the four winds. Furthermore she did not believe that I could possibly be safe on the mainland should there be a German invasion, even though I might be protected by Miss S. and the school, and instead earmarked a particular cliff overlooking the Bay of Port Erin from which – in the spirit of the zealots of Masada – we might make our final exit! This particular area was then still out of bounds for us, but one conjectured that in the desperate circumstances which might drive us to this dire end no one would object to our short-lived escape!

It was small wonder such thoughts crossed one's mind because for days on end one would hear in the evenings German planes overhead on their way to bomb Liverpool, with the drone that denoted heavy loads, whereas one could distinguish a different kind of sound when they returned with their bombs obviously discharged. One evening there was a commotion, possibly triggered by the noise of aeroplanes, when the two women we had suspected of being Nazi sympathisers rushed out on to the staircase shouting jubilantly that German parachutists were landing. In the event nothing more was heard in the camp and we had no means of knowing whether any Germans had in fact baled out from planes that might have been shot down. However the atmosphere had been electric, and the two women had revealed themselves, though, to give them the benefit of doubt, perhaps they were just excited at the prospect of seeing their own countrymen – or even possibly simply men – from whom they, as non-Jews, would have nothing to fear.

By way of entertainment and as a distraction from our many concerns, the different houses put on shows or concerts according to the particular talents of the inmates. As there was a curfew at 9 p.m. each house was limited to its own residents only, both from the point of view of performers and of audience. There were no great geniuses among us at the Strand Cafe, and without even a piano the scope of our offerings was very limited indeed and, I fear, lacked sparkle and wit, to say the least. There were some tolerably amusing skits and sketches, some readings, and my short 'act', for which I had been coached by the Hungarian girl who had some experience of theatre. It was the one and only appearance in my life as a soubrette, and the song and dance routine must have been pretty awful.

Such activities at least relieved the monotony of the autumn and winter months of 1940. The weather could be rather inhospitable with tearing storms and heavy rains, and sometimes it became almost impossible for the less robust to negotiate the rather steep stretch of road nearby. Yet the time did pass, and I myself was never bored, I had even enjoyed my fifteenth birthday that summer and never felt that the forebodings of the pessimists among us would be realised. To live from day to day without being able to plan ahead for a future so uncertain, and to be totally in the hands of distant, faceless men over whom one had no control was certainly demoralising at times. However, worse than anything was the knowledge that on the mainland England was suffering so at the hands of our enemies, and that we were precluded from sharing her hours of great trial.

That autumn the Day of Atonement – Yom Kippur – the most sacred day in the Jewish calendar, was observed in the local cinema turned synagogue. The auditorium was filled to overflowing and the nature of the liturgy, combined with the seriousness of the times, lent a profoundly moving effect to the service which visibly affected all, including those who were not normally deeply committed to, or observant of religious practices. Later on that year Christmas, in contrast, bore a distinctly secular air, and was attuned to the varying degrees of, or entire absence of, religious belief.

To mark the festive season, it was planned that a goose should be cooked. It had been no easy matter to procure the bird and it had required considerable powers of persuasion in order that our landlady might try and obtain it for us, a collection having been organised among the residents to meet the cost. The day arrived and the cooking, as usual, was begun with enthusiasm and in joyful anticipation of the end result. Alas, when the smells began to emanate from the kitchen the sense of glad expectancy changed to one of apprehension. When finally the bird was brought to the table and carved and shared, the reason soon became apparent. This goose was no gastronomic delight for she must have been fed on fish – herrings most likely (kippers, that is cured herrings, are a Manx speciality) – and the taste was horrid. Disappointment gave way to mirth and almost everyone took the spoilt Christmas dinner in good part.

The worries about the other members of the family weighed heavily on my mother, first and foremost the concern about Peter whose whereabouts were only guessed at according to whatever rumours were circulating at any given moment. Her sister and brother-in-law, her brother and his family, her mother were all caught in the Nazi web, the expansion of which was so frightening, and she, isolated as we were, unable to help them in any way. By comparison any privations we suffered were quite negligible. Once again in our lives, communications by post were what one lived for, day by day, and at last, early in March '41 came the longed-for letter which confirmed that Mother's vetting had, of course, been perfectly satisfactory, and in consequence we were to be released. What relief, what joy!

Our belongings were few so preparations and packing were soon accomplished, addresses were exchanged in the hope of keeping in touch with a few of the friends we had made, and then the day arrived when we left Port Erin to start the journey back to the mainland, this time a great deal more comfortably, looking forward to and wondering what our next home was going to be like. During our absence on the island our host family had moved from the Home Counties to the West of England, to the house of a relative, and we had no knowledge whatsoever about that part of the country, its geography or its people.

Chapter Six
Back to the Mainland

We arrived late in the evening in C. which, many, many years later in tourist brochures, was described as the jewel of the region, and from there proceeded by taxi to our destination. On the way I looked about me curiously but could discern nothing of the countryside, for it was dusk and moreover it seemed as though the area was enveloped in mist and fog. Only later was I to learn that what I took to be fog was in fact a smokescreen created by oil burning in bins all around an extensive airfield, to shroud it from view and save it from enemy bombs. On reaching the house we were received with kindness and were soon shown to our room, the lovely large dining room which had been made over to us, and without much further ado we gratefully prepared for bed.

The next morning, on waking up and going to the window, I was almost overwhelmed by the view over the beautiful garden which surrounded the house, and the gently rolling hills beyond, partly wooded, partly cultivated fields, a countryside not unlike the Vienna woods, and which looked almost unreal in its total contrast to the remoteness from the world in which we had lived those past months. So this was the place which was to be our new home then and – although I was not to know it at the time – the region of England which would be my home for all time.

I will call the house, built in the local traditional style, Woodcroft; it had become the refuge for many members of our hosts' family who had moved there to escape the bombing in the Home Counties. Amongst its new inhabitants were three charming, small children with their nanny, a most competent and cheerful Scotswoman; the children's mother, whose husband was in the army; and two very elderly ladies who stayed in their suite of rooms upstairs. Mother had a very busy life, cooking and keeping house for all and sundry, though there was one maidservant besides her. The niceties, if one can call them such, of differences of class were still observed, war or no war, and the little sitting room adjoining the kitchen was for our use and also served as the little children's dining room, where they were attended by their nanny.

Once settled into these new environs the question of what to do with me once more cropped up. How was I to continue with some kind of education and obtain qualifications which would enable me to seek work and earn my living? This last point was the one that concerned me the most, for I was not at all happy to be for ever an 'appendage', as I saw myself, to my mother, tolerated as a necessary evil in order that my mother's services might be retained. I had of course written to my form mistress at R. to tell her of our return to England, and once again she wanted me to come back to school so that I would be able to continue my studies and go for an Oxford scholarship. When Miss S. found herself in our part of the country she made a point of inviting Mother and myself to take tea with her at Maison Kunz in the elegant town some ten miles from where we lived, and there she personally put forward the idea, very charmingly and persuasively, that I should return to R. and live at her house. It was an uncomfortable meeting as far as I was concerned for I could sense a certain tension between the two women, both wishing to do the best for me. It was evident that Mother would not agree to such an arrangement, which I believe she felt would make her beholden to Miss S. Never one to take kindly to accepting charity of any sort, she thought that whatever she or I needed must be provided by herself, and that anything beyond her means was simply not to be contemplated.

Also ruled out was the other option of going to a local high school as that involved cost, and, furthermore, I could not bear the thought of joining youngsters my own age, feeling that with such experiences behind me I would not easily fit into their company, nor would I wish to be with my own age group and so have to attend school for two more years before taking the final examinations. I also explored the possibility of taking a course at a local technical college but rejected that because of the cost of bus fares and other expenses and in the end, after very careful consideration, chose to take a correspondence course, the only type of distance learning then available, with the University Correspondence College at Cambridge. The fees for such a course were manageable, and I could choose five subjects, namely English, mathematics (these two were mandatory) plus French, German and Latin, which would give me London matriculation. I was fairly confident that I could cope with studying these particular subjects on my own without outside help. I allowed myself ten months to achieve my goal.

It worked extremely well. I applied myself with a will and was happy to have my nose in books again, a wonderful sensation after the decidedly unacademic months I had spent. The system the college used I found excellent. Each week a block of work would come to me by post and each week I completed the papers set for homework, which I dispatched back to the tutors at the college who subsequently, and very promptly, returned them, corrected and annotated in the most helpful manner. I was able to shut myself away in our room to study, from which I emerged at more or less set times to lend a hand with housework, run errands or in other ways make myself useful. One of my most pleasant tasks was to fetch the milk from the nearby farm which I reached by walking across a field, singing most of the way. Life was good again and I felt lucky.

We now began to receive letters from Peter in Australia and knew that he was safe and that he would at the earliest possible moment try yet again to join the British army and return to the UK. We also had news via Sweden, where my Uncle Julius had had business dealings with a manufacturer of chocolate, that Aunt Adele and Uncle Hermann were still in Vienna, but at another address. Clearly they had also been evicted from their home and were now renting a furnished room. To this new address we were now able to send Red Cross messages from May until November 1941 and had messages back. These messages, both the outgoing and incoming ones, had to be restricted to twenty-five words and therefore could give no more than the barest, but for all that vital, information. At the end of 1941 these messages ceased, and it was not until September 1942 that we heard from them again, but now from Budapest. We were happy to think they might have found sanctuary there, but only learned at the end of the war how they had fared.

To begin with, when things in Vienna had reached the stage where they were in danger of being transported any day, Adele and Hermann decided to make for the Hungarian border, and there found someone who, in exchange for the last pieces of jewellery which had not been surrendered to the authorities as ordered, would take them across the frontier. They crossed at Sopron and made their way to the capital, where some cousins of my aunt might give them a little assistance. They had no papers but managed to get lodgings, where they kept themselves very much to themselves and subsisted on the very little money they had brought plus the earnings of my aunt, who was knitting and crocheting for a small handicraft shop where no one asked too many questions about her origins. She had a smattering of Hungarian, just enough to get by, and they both adapted to this hole-and-corner existence with their customary courageous optimism. After the annexation of Austria, when the systematic expropriation of Jewish people's property had first begun, I remember how my uncle, indicating the furniture, the glass and porcelain with an expansive gesture of the hand, had exclaimed, "Ballast, it's all ballast – one should be able to live without it all!" Evidently he lived according to these words when he and my aunt were reduced to such humble conditions and when possessions were their least concern, where danger lurked at every turn and the fear of betrayal was constantly with them.

In March 1944 Hungary, under the leadership of Admiral Horthy, threw in her lot with Germany, and the Germans took charge of the country. Now came the blackest time for them, and they knew that only the most carefully observed secrecy and the greatest amount of luck could save them from the daily round-ups and deportations, the dreaded actions of the Hungarian Arrow Cross movement,[*] which were now inexorably in progress. I remember my aunt saying how guilty she felt when, from their window, they saw in the street below a column of Jews being taken away, and how she had a great urge to rush down and join them. The instinct for survival prevailed though and they stayed and struggled on, and gradually they came to know that in the war on the eastern front the tide was beginning to turn and the victorious Russian army was marching west and sooner or later would enter Hungary, which would mean liberation for them, as for so many others.

---

[*] The Hungarian Arrow Cross organisation was the fascist movement given power by Horthy towards the latter part of the war. Their reign of terror left tens of thousands dead in the last few months of the war. See Paul Lendvai, *Hungary: The Art of Survival*, I.B. Tauris, pp.22 and 43.

She told us the story of how they lived in cellars during the siege and bombardment of Budapest, precariously and near to starvation, and how eventually in December 1944 the Soviets came and there were battles, street by street, and then soldiers came to their cellar – and how they were welcomed. They were a ragtag crew, who had clearly been fighting and suffering privations themselves for months, and many wanted drink at any price. They would lay their hands on anything that passed for alcohol, even methylated spirit or eau de cologne, and when drunk they were dangerous. My Uncle Hermann had to physically put himself between one of them and a young girl a soldier wanted to rape and indicated that only over his dead body might the deed be done. The soldier gave up, for it must be said that towards old people and children the Russian soldiers showed kindness.

The scant information which came to us via the Red Cross in 1942 allayed our worst fears and anxieties because Mother knew that at least her beloved sister and her husband were alive, even though we could then only guess at their circumstances and struggles. Of the other members of the family, those left in Czechoslovakia, we knew nothing after the initial messages through the Swedish contact ceased. As far as I was concerned, being young and with a lot of study to pursue purposefully towards my objective of becoming independent, I was able to put these cares to one side and in fact enjoy very much our new surroundings. There was country dancing every week in the garage, made available to the local village people by our hosts; there were new faces; and there was a wonderful sense of camaraderie which seemed to have been brought about by the war, by shared concerns and shortages and by the knowledge that nearly everyone suffered from the inevitable separation of families, not to mention the tragedies of loss and bereavement. The German language was taboo for us and Mother and I always spoke English, even when we were alone. She worked hard, as always, and fulfilled her role as housekeeper and friend to all at Woodcroft with dignity and skill, and created good, wholesome meals imaginatively, notwithstanding the scarcity of materials on account of rationing.

In the summer of 1941 I had my sixteenth birthday, and on reaching this mature age my status as an alien had to be defined by the authorities. I was summoned to attend a session of the tribunal created for that purpose in Bristol, and mother and I made the journey by train. On the way she tried to reassure me and told me not to worry, and the more she said, the more nervous and apprehensive I became. When finally I entered the sanctum of the law courts where the hearing before magistrates, most likely, was to take place, I was totally bemused and my replies to questions came in a hoarse whisper because my voice almost failed me. Their worships must soon have come to the conclusion that this was no potential Mata Hari before them for my ordeal was soon over, I was dismissed, and my voice returned as if by magic. Before long I received notification that I was now classed a 'refugee from Nazi oppression' and would not hear the epithet 'enemy alien' applicable to those deemed not to be in opposition to the Nazi regime.

Winter came and with the new year of '42 the news that Peter would soon be returning. My arrangements and entry application for the matriculation examination had then to be made also, and I began to get excited at the prospect of bringing my studies to their culmination. Meanwhile I had bought a shorthand manual and was teaching myself Pitman's shorthand and through the kindness of the local vicar was allowed to practise typing on his old machine. This way no extra expense would need to be incurred for the acquisition of these skills for I was ever aware of the importance of being economical, knowing how Mother wanted to be in a position to be of help to Peter when he returned from Australia, penniless and practically destitute.

Chapter Seven

Peter Returns

It was a wonderful coincidence that Peter actually came back at the very time we found ourselves in London for my examination. Somehow or other our reunion took place in a street in central London, and it was unbelievably poignant. I had to fight back the tears and Mother had difficulty controlling her emotion, but one didn't want to make an exhibition of oneself, having learned and, up to a point, admired the English stiff upper lip! It was to a Lyons Corner House that we repaired to celebrate Peter's return over welcome cups of tea and buns which were within our means. Now we were to hear just a little of his adventures, but more pressing were his immediate plans, which were to report to the military authorities for his first posting as a soldier with the Pioneer Corps, the only part of the British Army in which Austrian and German refugees were then allowed to serve.

In order to make the most of our brief sojourn in London, and to make up for the dearth of cultural activities in our lives, we managed to fit in a visit to the National Gallery where regular lunchtime concerts, tickets costing one shilling, were given by great artists, notwithstanding the bombing of the capital. It was a memorable occasion and to see men and women in uniform and civilians mingling to take time off from the war, so to speak, and share the experience of beautiful music was intensely moving and uplifting. Dame Myra Hess played Beethoven, and we were thankful that the wailing of air raid sirens did not just then interrupt the near-religious atmosphere which prevailed.

As far as I remember the time was all too short in which we could reminisce and bring one another up to date with what had happened in our respective lives. It must be said that at that time Peter didn't give us an inkling of the more dreadful things he had endured; of these he spoke only much later, and then rarely, when the passing of years had softened the hurt and when perhaps subsequent happier events had served to redress the balance. He was once heard to remark, though, that he had gone out (to Australia) a boy and returned a man. Before long he adjusted to the new life of a soldier and was happy now to belong to HM British Army, albeit to a non-combatant section whose task was in the main to perform the less desirable work, such as the setting up of camp sites, digging trenches, making latrines and the thousand and one mundane and disagreeable, but nonetheless necessary jobs which are all part and parcel of the activities within the services.

Later on during the war he satisfied his wish to participate in a fighting unit and volunteered, as soon as it was permitted, for service in the Parachute Regiment, underwent the arduous training and looked fit and strikingly handsome. He then had to change his name to an Anglicised version so that, in case of being taken prisoner by the Germans, his true origins might be concealed. In the event, thank God, that event never occurred, and he served during the rest of the war with distinction in the Sixth Airborne Division, taking part in the dropping over the Rhine when he sustained minor injuries.

The results of my matriculation examination were not long coming and I was exultant on hearing that I had passed in what was termed the first division, indicating that I had obtained top marks in all the five subjects. On hearing of my success, an acquaintance from my Isle of Man days, a Miss F., who was a teacher in Oxford and had taken a kindly interest in me, even entertaining me in her home one weekend, wanted me to try for a scholarship to the University of Oxford and would have liked to point me in the right direction. Once again such overtures were resisted for pecuniary reasons, and instead I resigned myself once and for all to becoming a working girl.

With matriculation coupled with a moderate skill in shorthand and typing and a glowing letter of reference from dear Miss S., my erstwhile form mistress, I felt suitably equipped to launch myself on a career and set forth to find a job. It was not very difficult in those days to find employment; after all the men and boys of military age were for the most part in the forces, as were indeed many women. What are nowadays called job centres were then known as labour exchanges, and one was to be found in every town in the country. I took myself to one of these and found there on the staff a most helpful and pleasant woman who suggested two or three possible positions for which I might apply. The one I settled for and which appealed to me most was a clerical job as office junior in the office of the local newspaper where I duly presented myself for interview. The editor himself, a quite elderly distinguished-looking gentleman, questioned me and examined my credentials and gave me the post there and then at a starting salary of thirty shillings a week.

My first impression, I distinctly remember, of the office was that I had stepped back in time, into a bygone era – the tall 'counting house' stools, the high sloping desks and antiquated wall cabinets which housed the enormously large, cumbersome ledgers, as they were called, all looked unmistakably like those depicted in old editions of Dickens. The secretary was ensconced in one part of the office – cubicle would be a more apt way of describing it – where she kept the books in neat, impeccable handwriting and where her authority was unquestioned. My own domain adjoined hers, much smaller, but similarly furnished with a desk and stool, the latter again without any backrest, which discouraged one from taking one's ease. I was considerably in awe of my superior, a lady totally dedicated to her work, of somewhat forbidding aspect, who neither in dress or hairstyle made any concessions to femininity or to pleasing the opposite sex. The experience of having me as an office junior must have been as peculiar to her as it was to me, but she was straightforward in her dealings with me and outlined my tasks, which were easy enough though not inspiring.

In my capacity as office junior I had to deal with customers bringing in advertisements, and these had to be appropriately charged for according to classification and length; I had to look after the stamps and keep exact account of them down to the last half penny; I had to address wrappers for newspapers which were dispatched by post; and on Fridays, when the paper 'came out', I had to sell them to customers who called in person to collect their copy. It was not without interest getting to recognise the faces of the business people in the town, the estate agents, the heads of private schools, the tradespeople and shop assistants, and in this way come face to face with a cross-section of the community. There were moments of quiet, unintended humour too, such as when so-called 'In Memoriam' notices were brought in for insertion in the appropriate columns. These were intended to commemorate loved ones on the anniversaries of their deaths and were couched in poetic language, frequently of the surviving members of the family's own devising. One such verse remembered the dear departed spouse with the following words:

> No more suffering, no more pain
> 'Till some day we meet again.

Before very long the somewhat boring routine of the office was relieved when the editor began to give me snippets of information to 'knock into shape', that is to say to write them up for publication. It was a new experience to see my humble efforts appear in print the following week and I was pleased. Having decided that my English was good enough and that I could put words together, the editor offered to transfer me to the editorial department where I was to assist the sub-editor, a genial, local man who seemed to know everything about everyone in the little town! He was considerably overworked, having lost all the young men in his department who had gone off to the war, so he was pleased to have me and I was delighted with the promotion and gladly made way for a new, hapless office junior to step into my place.

This was the beginning of more interesting work, and Mr F. who always addressed me as 'Miss' – there was not then the familiarity of first names among members of staff – took me round at first in the battered old van which was the firm's property to introduce me to 'district' news gathering. This meant scouring the outlying villages, calling on members of the clergy and using them and local newsagents as prime sources of information on deaths, marriages and so forth, then following these up and collecting what details one could. There were harrowing moments when one learned of the death on active service of soldiers, airmen and sailors, and inevitably one's heart went out to the bereaved. Normal deaths, that is deaths from old age, were not so sad, and I became accustomed to attending funerals, taking names of mourners at the church door and even making notes of the inscriptions on wreaths at the graveside. Calling on the families on occasions such as these could be difficult, and I remember finding it not a little awkward, on being invited to view the body of one deceased who was laid out in the front parlour, to get out of joining the family and drinking tea with them without giving offence.

Gradually many other duties came my way – the reporting of social events, garden parties (to raise funds for this or that war effort), district council meetings, police court (as the magistrates' court was then called), county court proceedings (which mostly dealt with debts or rent disputes), but, best of all things musical, wonderful concerts given by famous artists under the auspices of CEMA, the Council for the Encouragement of Music and the Arts.

Invariably the task of reporting these events was assigned to me, and I must confess that my enthusiasm far exceeded my knowledge of the subject, but with the aid of reference books and – as it seems to me in retrospect – not a small measure of hubris, I managed to cobble together reviews, one could hardly call them critiques, which were found to be acceptable and on occasions even earned me praise. The drab surroundings of a local church hall were given an aura of splendour and nobility when such artists as Benno Moiseiwitsch, Pouishnoff or Eileen Joyce came to play. There was a peculiar poignancy to Eileen Joyce's performance, for she had only just heard that her husband, a Royal Air Force pilot, had been reported missing. The kind of feelings evoked by that and so many other tragedies of the time are similar to those stirred by the following letter, which appeared in *The Times* of June 18th, 1940, together with some introductory paragraphs:

Reprinted from The Times, *June 18, 1940*

An Airman To His Mother

The Fight with Evil

"My Earthly Mission is Fulfilled"

Among the personal belongings of a young R.A.F. pilot in a Bomber Squadron who was recently reported "Missing, believed killed", was a letter to his mother – to be sent to her if he were killed.

"This letter was perhaps the most amazing one I have ever read; simple and direct in its wording but splendid and uplifting in its outlook," says the young officer's station commander. "It was inevitable that I should read it – in fact he must have intended this, for it was left open in order that I might be certain that no prohibited information was disclosed.

"I sent the letter to the bereaved mother, and asked her whether I might publish it anonymously, as I feel its contents may bring comfort to other mothers, and that every one in our country may feel proud to read of the sentiments which support 'an average airman' in the execution of his present arduous duties. I have received the mother's permission, and I hope this letter may be read by the greatest possible number of our countrymen at home and abroad."

Text of the letter

Dearest Mother – Though I feel no premonition at all, events are moving rapidly, and I have instructed that this letter be forwarded to you should I fail to return from one of the raids which we shall shortly be called upon to undertake. You must hope on for a month, but at the end of that time you must accept the fact that I have handed my task over to the extremely capable hands of my comrades of the Royal Air Force, as so many splendid fellows have already done.

First, it will comfort you to know that my role in this war has been of the greatest importance. Our patrols far out over the North Sea have helped to keep the trade routes clear for our convoys and supply ships, and on one occasion our information was instrumental in saving the lives of the men in a crippled lighthouse relief ship. Though it will be difficult for you, you will disappoint me if you do not at least try to accept the facts dispassionately, for I shall have done my duty to the utmost of my ability. No man can do more, and no one calling himself a man could do less.

I have always admired your amazing courage in the face of continual setbacks; in the way you have given me as good an education and background as anyone in the country; and always kept up appearances without ever losing faith in the future. My death would not mean that your struggle has been in vain. Far from it. It means that your sacrifice is as great as mine. Those who serve England must expect nothing from her; we debase ourselves if we regard our country as merely a place in which to eat and sleep.

History resounds with illustrious names who have given all, yet their sacrifice has resulted in the British Empire, where there is a measure of peace, justice, and freedom for all, and where a higher standard of civilisation has evolved, and is still evolving, than anywhere else. But this is not only concerning our own land. Today we are faced with the greatest organised challenge to Christianity and civilisation that the world has ever seen, and I count myself lucky and honoured to be the right age and fully trained to throw my full weight into the scale. For this I have to thank you. Yet there is more work for you to do. The home front will still have to stand united for years after the war is won. For all that can be said against it, I still maintain that this war is a very good thing; every individual is having the chance to give and dare all for his principle like the martyrs of old. However long time may be, one thing can never be altered — I shall have lived and died an

Englishman. Nothing else matters one jot, nor can anything ever change it.

You must not grieve for me, for if you really believe in religion and all that it entails that would be hypocrisy. I have no fear of death; only a queer elation... I would have it no other way. The universe is so vast and so ageless that the life of one man can only be justified by the measure of his sacrifice. We are sent to this world to acquire a personality and a character to take with us that can never be taken from us. Those who just eat and sleep, prosper and procreate are no better than animals if all their lives they are at peace.

I firmly and absolutely believe that evil things are sent into the world to try us; they are sent deliberately by our Creator to test our mettle because He knows what is good for us. The Bible is full of cases where the easy way out has been discarded for moral principles.

I count myself fortunate in that I have seen the whole country and known men of every calling. But with the final test of war I consider my character fully developed. Thus at my early age my earthly mission is already fulfilled and I am prepared to die with just one regret, and one only – that I could not devote myself to making your declining years more happy by being with you; but you will live in peace and freedom and I shall have directly contributed to that, so here again my life will not have been in vain.

Your loving Son,

*

When it came to the reporting of formal events which had to do with local authorities, I recall with gratitude and affection being taken under the wings of one particular colleague from another newspaper who never failed to give help, advice and encouragement. He and others frequently took me along in the mornings to drink coffee, discuss work and gossip in the little back parlour of a local baker's shop where the hospitality that was dispensed was cordial and the coffee, though questionable in its quality, was always conducive to relaxed enjoyment.

Back in the office and busy at the typewriter, one worked much of the time against the background noise and clatter of a linotype machine, long since outdated and overtaken by modern technology and computerised printing equipment. One particular operator, who was in charge of the biggest and noisiest machine two rooms away from mine, had shown himself friendly and had even invited me, together with a friend, to tea at his cottage where he and his wife, who were childless, lived with an aunt. He was a North Country man, rough in appearance but, as I thought, with his heart in the right place. His attitude towards me underwent a complete change and turned to vitriolic hostility after I wrote a commentary on a publication by Victor Gollancz which dealt with the tragedy of Jews in Nazi Germany. My editor from time to time received information about new books that were coming out and reviewed them in our paper. On this occasion he passed on to me the extract, which he evidently considered I would be able to write about with some conviction, and I set about it with great earnestness and endeavoured to produce a few paragraphs that might be worthy of the subject. So far as I remember he changed not a word, and what appeared in the paper was the following article:

"LET MY PEOPLE GO"

A Tragedy of Today

Victor Gollancz's Pamphlet

"Yea, truth and justice then
will down return to men
Orbed in a rainbow; and like glories wearing,
Mercy will sit between,
Throned in celestial sheen,

With radiant feet and tissued clouds down
steering;
And Heaven as at some festival,
Will open wider the gates of her high palace
hall."

Amid the peace, today, of the Berkshire
countryside (and incidentally the Gloucestershire
countryside too), it is difficult not to feel that
there is something about Britain – whether it be
her fortunate history, with its long record of
democracy, however imperfect, or whether it be
that peculiar combination of gentleness and
unsentimentality which is characteristic of her
people – that specially fits her to play a most
noble part in rebuilding our shattered world.
But history does not forgive lost opportunities,
whether in the moulding of national character or
in the determination of events. If now, in this
moment of agony for millions of fellow human
beings the British people, feeling its
responsibility as a democracy, chooses the
positive path of mercy for the persecuted rather
than the merely negative one of retribution for
the persecutors, then it will be bringing nearer
the day when the words of Milton's hymns, "On
the morning of Christ's Nativity," will have
their true significance.

TAKE ACTION

These exactly are the words of Victor
Gollancz in his pamphlet entitled "Let my
People Go" which appeared on Christmas Day,
1942, and which, although widely read, has not
yet had the wanted effect. It is spontaneity that
has often before furthered a cause and surely,
when we think of all the causes that deserve

furthering we must consider that of providing a refuge for people that are being persecuted in a way that has no predecessor in history. To linger and wait, while millions that might be saved, who are on our side in this gigantic struggle, are suffering physical and mental agony, is unforgivable. Action, prompted by the latest outbursts of inhuman callousness and fiendishness, ought to be taken at once. It would be a noble work that would shed greater glory on the pages of British history and you, men and women of Britain, would feel pangs of regret if help were denied to innocent people who were Hitler's first victims in his enormous book of oppression and attack and if his planned extermination of the Jewish people on the continent were achieved without your striving to prevent it.

SYMPATHY INSUFFICIENT

I speak as one of those fortunate people who escaped from that cauldron of hell, Europe, to find peace of mind in England. That peace of mind is profoundly shaken by events that are heart-breaking to us who, with some experience of cruel Nazi rule, fully realise to what the latest outbursts amount to. Wherever I went and touched upon the subject I encountered sympathy, sincere and heart-felt. But now we want more than that. Dare those who have the power refuse to do everything they humanly can? "A country," writes Mrs Blanche Dugdale, in the Spectator, "that does not open its doors to those who are hunted by murderers participates in the crime." This is a serious accusation, but nevertheless a true one.

Let me now dwell on the actual happenings that make our hearts go out to those in hopeless distress. Let everyone conjure up their picture of horrors as far as they can imagine. Enough information is given on the wireless and through those formations who have the up-to-date reports of atrocities. Let it be enough to say that help is absolutely urgent and that it is almost, but only almost, too late.

AN APPEAL

It is a difficult task upon which we are to embark, but the ultimate object, that of saving martyrs, is a shining aim. Most of us have not the power to materialise so ambitious a scheme as the organised rescue work of those people trapped in Europe. But they have another important power – the power of influence, and that, for the good of the cause, they ought to practise. Don't wash your hands of the responsibility – it would be contrary to British tradition – but in your own sphere of life try to kindle a spirit that will not allow fellow human beings to go on being tortured to death. This is an earnest appeal to everyone to perform an act of humanity which is worthy of every effort.

The publication of this article, insignificant though it undoubtedly was, helped to make me feel I was doing something worthwhile. I had considered joining the services in order to contribute more directly, as I thought, to the war effort, but was dissuaded from such an idea by my editor, who assured me that my work was valuable, and that it was in fact rated as war work in lieu of service in the forces or the alternatives open to women, namely work in factories, on the land or in hospitals.

Friends of mine worked in the local nursery caring for very small children whose mothers could not, for a variety of reasons, care for them during certain hours of the day or night. Through them I learned something of the little mites' background, as for example of one mother who had committed the 'sin' – as it was regarded then – of having an illegitimate child, but not only that, an illegitimate child by a black American soldier. The baby was adorable and was the darling of the young girls who looked after him. Society generally, however, was not so understanding and girls who erred from the paths of conventional respectability did not have an easy time.

There were the sad cases of girls becoming involved with servicemen from overseas, marrying in good faith, and finding out too late that the marriage had been contracted bigamously. We knew of one such case where a young woman, who had graduated in French, married an officer in the Free French forces. Unfortunately the word 'free' only applied to his military status. Against such instances, generally speaking, there were many more felicitous associations, sometimes tragically cut short by death in active service. The term 'sweetheart' was much in use, applicable to either sex, and was indicative of tender, romantic love. The word 'boyfriend' meant exactly that – a friend who was a boy rather than a girl; the word 'partner' signified a business connection, and marriage was still regarded by almost everyone as the natural and proper culmination of a loving relationship.

The time had now come for us to make an all-out effort to establish for ourselves a home we could call our own, to break away from our host family and to find accommodation of some sort to rent. Easier said than done. The first hurdle was finding such a place at a rent which, by pooling our wages, my mother and I could afford. Flats or apartments in the way these terms are understood nowadays were unobtainable to anyone as impecunious as ourselves. The best one might hope for were some rooms with shared amenities. We thought we had succeeded in securing such lodgings in an excellent solid-looking stone house where a splendid walnut tree stood sentinel in the garden and where the lady proprietor showed pleasure at the prospect of having us as tenants, only to have our hopes dashed by the billeting officer, who was empowered to grant or withhold his consent. It was his duty in those wartime years to restrict the best available accommodation for personnel engaged in war work, people who had come specifically to the area for the purpose of such work, and who consequently were to be given priority.

This disappointment we had to take in our stride. Eventually we found another place, rooms in a large house which, putting it mildly, had seen better days and was divided up into what were euphemistically called 'flats', ours consisting of one vast room, originally the billiard room, a small bedroom and a moderately sized kitchen which sported an ancient gas cooker and a small sink with one cold tap. This then was to be our home for the foreseeable future. From a most unprepossessing dwelling it was transformed into a passably acceptable human habitation by dint of hard work. Walls had to be whitewashed, floors to be scrubbed and stained, some kind of curtains to be hung, though material was virtually unobtainable, and some household utensils acquired, a formidable task when all goods were in such short supply.

Once we had got the place shipshape, or as shipshape as it was possible to make it, and there was a fire lit in the grate, it was almost cosy, at least so it appeared to us, and it seemed blissful to have, for the first time since emigrating, four walls to ourselves. How pleasurable to be able to invite friends notwithstanding the humbleness of the premises, to come and go as we pleased, to have a life not bound to our hosts and their particular needs and demands. This was a period of comparative calm for us when we were yet hopeful that our dear ones in occupied Europe might somehow or other survive and be reunited with us. The harsh reality was still to be revealed.

Chapter Eight

Terrible Truths

In August '43 we had sent the Red Cross message, a facsimile of which is shown at the end of the photograph section, to Hungary to Aunt and Uncle, who went under the assumed name of Barcs Tiborne to hide their true identity, and received their reply which indicated that not only they, but my Uncle Julius's family were then safe also.

It transpired later, however, that they were not well informed. As news came out of Europe with the advance of the Allied armies and tales of unbelievable horror were gradually confirmed, our fears for them grew steadily more intense. Their younger daughter Marietta had been the only member of their family to escape to England in the summer of '39 and had been received into an English family. She trained as a nurse and returned to Czechoslovakia in order to try and trace her parents and sister Edith. What happened to them is best told in the letter she wrote to us. This is the letter:

Tuesday, 10th July 1945

...Now I am back in this wonderful country and I love it even more than before. I have even greater faith in its future. We shall start again and we can do it again. The future has got to be better and what has happened must always be remembered and be a warning to us all. But we know all that and so there is no need for me to preach.

I know that you are anxious to know whom I have found of my people. My parents are both dead. My mother was sent into a gas chamber in Poland and my father died somewhere in a concentration camp. There is no need for me to add anything to this, you know my feelings. My only consolation is that my mother didn't suffer as she was murdered immediately she arrived in Poland. What my father went through, I don't know, and what sort of a death met him is also not known. I hope you received my telegram, in which I told you that I found Edith. Here is her experience. As you know they were here in Teresin until October 1944. She became a nurse in the hospital where I am working now. She said life here was bearable, later on she thought of Teresin as a Paradise. This was a Ghetto where Jews could live quite freely and worked. The accommodation was pretty awful and food very rare. But they were allowed to produce plays, have concerts and dances. As you can imagine there were a lot of famous people, such as actors, musicians, doctors, etc. My sister was very ill, had encephalitis (inflammation of the brain) and was operated on, had a Mastoidectomy and from that had facial paralysis on one side of her face. She is still paralysed a little but there is apparently hope of a complete cure. It was all a matter of life and death and she got married to this lawyer while seriously ill in hospital. I've heard that he was a very nice and popular person and they were very much in love with each other. My sister got well at last but wasn't able to work in the hospital any more. She was put to work on the land instead. Her married life lasted all together eight months. She said in spite of being in camp, it was the happiest period of her life. My parents also loved him and my mother spoilt him as if he was her own son. Edith said he had always so much faith in the future, he used to cheer everybody. His parents were also here and Edith is very fond of them. Funnily enough, they come from the same town as we went to school. Anyway, beginning of October he and my father were put in a transport and sent to Osvedein in Poland. Edith heard that the next transport was to follow them and they could be with them and so she and Mother and hundreds of other women, who all wanted to follow their menfolk, volunteered. Edith says, imagine the irony of it all, they all absolutely fought to go. They got together all the food they could get to bring with them and they sang all the way and laughed. But, of course, it was all a trick. They landed somewhere quite different and were immediately ordered to get out and leave everything behind. Then they were selected. Edith went on one side, my mother on the other. They didn't only separate them because of their age, it just depended who they took a fancy to. Edith wanted to stay with Mother, but they told her it didn't matter for they would see each other in the evening. Later she found out that all women with Mother went immediately into gas chambers. All women with children were also gassed. Edith and the other women were marched away, stripped and shaved all over. They were given one part of some clothing. For instance, if they had a petticoat, they weren't allowed anything else. The things were all filthy and lousy. Each morning Edith had to stand on guard four hours in the cold, dressed in just a summer frock, torn in the front. Then she was marched four miles to work in a munitions factory where she had to stand all the day. In the evening she was marched back again and had four hours on guard. She lived on one plate of watery soup all day. They slept on a narrow wooden plank with no blankets or anything. The filth and lousiness was terrible. Of course, there was no sanitation whatsoever. I forgot to tell you that my sister was pregnant. She had to hide that, as they killed all pregnant women or operated on them, without anaesthetic, of course, and then murdered them. There were some Italian prisoners near by and once they threw her a piece of bread which she picked up. An S.S. woman saw her and gave her such a slap that she knocked a tooth out. You see they had S.S. women over them, all young girls of 20 or so, all of them sexual maniacs and such horrible beasts. The things they did are unbelievable. At the end they discovered that she was pregnant and sent her to Belsen. On the way, something went wrong and the transport stopped half-way. Then came the Russians and they liberated them. She spent some time in a German house and then she started on her journey to Prague with a French prisoner of war on a horse cart. Edith was then in her ninth month of pregnancy. When they got to Prague she had to be taken straight to the hospital where she gave birth to a baby boy. She had a very difficult birth and although the child was quite normal it had cerebral haemorrhage and died the fifth day. Edith then looked for news of her husband and parents, or should I say father, as she knew Mother was dead.

Quite by chance she met a nurse from Teresin, whom she knew from olden days and whom I got to know the previous day in the hospital. I had asked her, the way I asked everybody here, if she knew my parents and sister and luckily she knew my sister very well. They all know and like Edith in the hospital. Doctors and nurses alike. Well it so happened the following day this nurse went to Prague and saw my sister in a restaurant and, of course, ran to her and told her I was here. Edith looked at her daft like and told her not to be silly, I was in England. Half an hour later she found out that her husband died of Typhus in a camp. She then came straight to Teresin and found me in the dining room. Walked to me and said, "I am Edith, remember me?" I shall never forget the way she looked, all the misery and unhappiness in the world was pictured in her face. She was small and somehow shrunken, and in her face was only bitterness and irony. Her voice was full of that irony too. Having one side of her face paralysed added to that sarcastic expression. Her hair was short, of course, and fair and also her eyebrows and eyelashes were fair. She used to be darker than I. But it was my Edith and I had her back again and I thanked God for her. I had lost hope of seeing my parents again but I always felt that I'd find Edith. Now I know why I wanted to come back so soon, it was God's will, for I know that my sister wouldn't have wanted to live any more, she would never have got over that last shock of knowing her husband was dead. She said that the only reason she endured and lived through everything was because she always believed she would be reunited with her husband. Now she has at least me and I know I can restore new hope and faith into her and already she is gradually becoming her old self again.

Wednesday, 11th July

...I know I haven't said anything of my impressions yet. What should I say more than that I like it all very much. I really feel at home and Prague is even more beautiful than I thought, and my, my, what a lot of good-looking people! They are very well dressed. Real

smart, I feel awful as I have nothing but my uniform and cannot wait until they send on my case which is stored by the firm Pickfords in London. Poor Edith has nothing and I haven't much more here. Still, we'll manage. Food is terribly scarce, everything on points, and shops are empty. But slowly one can already notice how things are getting back to normal. Cigarettes are gold, I gave all mine to Edith as she is still a very heavy smoker. Milk in Prague is a rare thing, only mothers with babies get this. Here in Teresin, food is quite plentiful as, of course, all the best comes here. I think I am even fatter and sunburnt. The weather is wonderful and the country round here is so beautiful and picturesque that it takes my breath away. The River Labe is so broad and lovely, I couldn't resist swimming in it. Well, you needn't worry about me. I feel full of energy into the future and in spite of everything I don't feel lonely or unhappy.

Subsequently my cousin told me of how she had met a survivor who had known her father and had told her a little more; that my uncle, together with others, had tried to escape, but that he had a poisoned foot, so walking was difficult, running impossible, and in consequence his attempt had failed. She also told me of the faithful servant Pepicka, who had been in the family home in Rohatec when she was a child, of her devotion to the family and in particular to her mother, who had befriended her and treated her like a daughter. Pepicka, during the Terezin years, had smuggled food parcels into the camp. Later Marietta had had a moving reunion with Pepicka, then aged eighty, when she had returned to Czechoslovakia. On this occasion she had made a pilgrimage to her village where my Uncle Julius and Aunt Bertha – she had worked together with other women to improve the living conditions and to care for the sick in their community – are remembered. Their names, together with the names of others who lost their lives in the Second World War, are inscribed on a monument erected in the village square.

Many years later letters that my Uncle Julius had written in 1942 and 1943 came into my possession. In the letter dated July '42 (see Figure 2 and 2a) and which apparently was routed via Sweden, he writes of having to 'register' for the *Übersiedlung* (moving house!), but that after having first been postponed for four weeks, he now anticipated the move would take place in September, barring a miracle. The first stage, he continues, is Theresienstadt (Terezin), and thence presumably further. He refers to his aunt, my grandmother's sister Minna, having been 'taken away' (the letter altogether had had to be couched in covert language). He also describes how it had not surprised him, that a cousin had written to say that it was now the turn of the (Jewish) old people's homes (in Vienna) and, he adds, that such was also the case there (in Czechoslovakia). He thanks God that He had taken his mother (my grandmother) to Himself in time. He further mentions one 'Rudi', who he assumed would be spared transportation so long as he lived with his Aryan wife in the same domicile, adding in realistic vein that he wondered how this marriage would survive.

In the letter dated 6th January, 1943 (see Figure 3, 3a, 3b and 3c) he writes, '...we are ready and are preparing ourselves feverishly. There is no sense in wasting too many words about what is inevitable... When we register we will be told our transport numbers, which I will let you know immediately. These numbers are very important for communicating because the address must contain this number. The address until further notice will be Theresienstadt, Post Bauschowitz. Gift parcels are permitted... There is no cause for concern if you receive neither letters nor cards after the confirmation of receipt [of parcels], as according to our information up to date this is not allowed... Josef writes that you worry about us. My dear, you don't help us in that way, it will only affect your health. Join your prayers with ours. May the Almighty keep us in good health and bring us together again...'

In the letter dated 22nd January, 1943 (see Figure 4, 4a and 4b) he begins, '*Nun ist es so weit*' (This is it), and continues that on the following day they start their journey. He gives the number of the transport, asks for news to be written on postcards only and says that no one should worry about them if they don't hear, though he promises to do his best in that respect. He asks that this news should be passed on to my side of the family and says 'we are calm and composed. We do not despair but have only one wish in this fateful hour, to remain in good health... '*Gott mit Euch und mit uns Allen*' – may God be with you and with us all.'

When my uncle and his family had had to leave the house in Rohatec where Peter and I had spent so many happy, sunny holidays, he made arrangements for Grandmother to go into a Jewish old people's home in Prague which was then still run by the Jewish community. They too had moved to Prague to await further developments and had frequently visited Grandmother. In some of her extant letters she speaks only of her longing for her children, never complains and puts her trust in God. In November 1941 she died, they said peacefully, in her sleep. There is a letter of condolence (refer to Figure 5) written to my Aunt Adele who was at that time still in Vienna, informing her of her mother's death. The writers must have been friends of my aunt's, for it is not a formal notification but begins with the words 'And so a faithful soul has passed away, a true heart no longer beats...' After giving more details about Grandmother's last hours and the affectionate comments of the nursing sister who had cared for her, only in the last paragraph does the writer refer to the transports and the need to be prepared, and the husband in a brief postscript reports that his eldest brother and his wife were taken away in the third transport and that he had no news of Hanna and Grete (presumably other close relatives).

Some doubt was cast in later years on the way Grandmother and possibly others in the home had ended their lives. We heard a rumour that their end had been hastened – very wisely if that was indeed the case – by the administration of increased dosages of sleeping drugs, thus forestalling their forcible removal and transportation, which was imminent. Mercifully she was not aware of the terror that reigned and was spared the agonies endured by others.

Gradually, with the end of the war, approaching news trickled through from various sources. As my cousin Marietta had gone back to Czechoslovakia with the Red Cross, so had others joined voluntary organisations with the object of helping but at the same time also finding out about what had befallen their families. One such was a friend of mine who went to Germany with this aim in view and was good enough to locate my cousin Ernestine, the daughter of my father's sister. She had never emigrated, had been classed by the Nazis as a 'half-Jew' and had spent the war on the 'other' side, so to speak, very much discriminated against, but on the whole safe. We had always nurtured the hope that her mother would have the protection of the 'Aryan' father and were therefore dismayed to learn that tragically she had not survived. Yes – *Onkel Hans* had in fact looked after his wife honourably but had become very ill with heart trouble, from which he died in December '44. His last two days the couple spent closely together in their home. Some three months after his death my aunt was summoned to Gestapo headquarters in Karlsbad, where they lived, and told to be ready for transportation to Theresienstadt within days. She decided – amid what turbulent feelings one can only imagine – that she would prefer to take her own life. To this end she took all that remained of her late husband's medication – her last request to her daughter was to bring her an old prayer book which had belonged to her own mother and which she herself, not having been a practising Jew for many years, had scarcely ever used.

Ironically, at the end of the war, when Czechoslovakia was liberated from the Germans, the Sudeten Germans as they were called, that is the ethnic Germans who lived, and had long lived, in the German-speaking part of the country – all of which had formerly been part of the Austro-Hungarian Empire – were expelled and repatriated to Germany. My cousin Ernestine and her half-sister were among these, forced to leave with just fifty kilograms of their possessions. They had a very hard time at first and were not welcomed by their new German neighbours. Eventually they managed to create new lives for themselves.

Aunt Adele and Uncle Hermann returned to a heavily scarred, bomb-damaged Vienna from Budapest. By then my uncle was a sick man since the nature of the lives they had been forced to live had taken its toll and he was suffering from heart trouble. The drugs he needed and which would certainly have prolonged his life were not available and, try as we might, we were unable to send them. He died then not long afterwards, happy to be liberated, yet a victim of his times.

Of many others – cousins, distant relatives and acquaintances – one never knew much except that they had disappeared and not been heard of again. Their fate and sufferings are not individually recorded but have become part of the wider history of the Holocaust.

My own odyssey here comes to an end. My days as a refugee were drawing to a close at the end of the war and for me there was a new beginning.

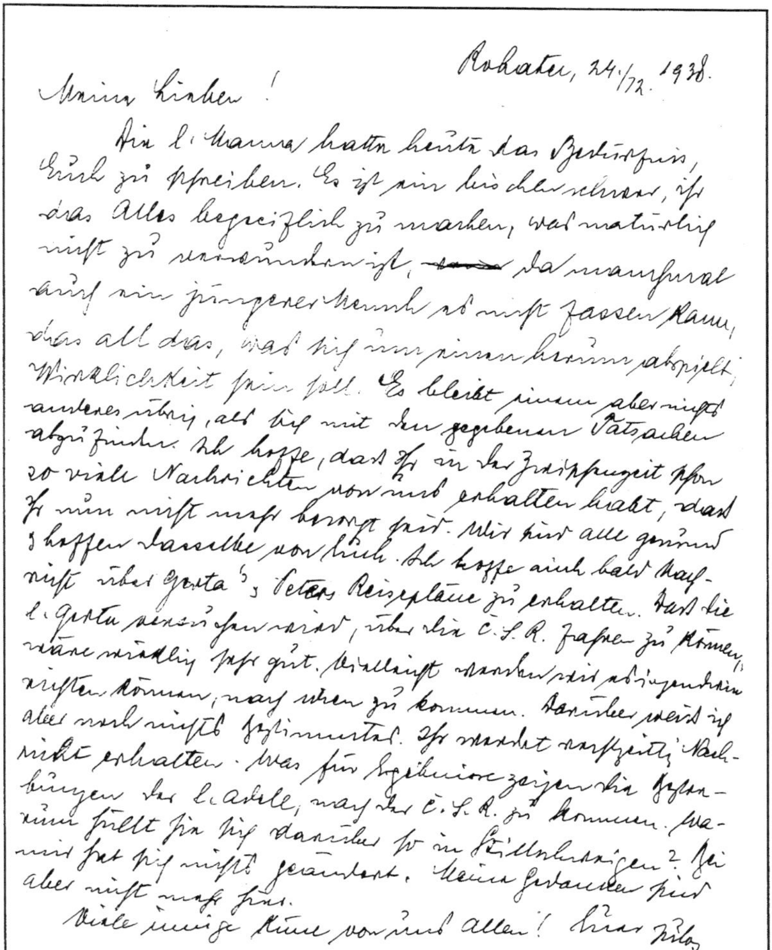

Rohatec, 24/12. 1938.

Meine Lieben!

Die l. Mama hatte heute das Bedürfnis, Euch zu schreiben. Es ist ein bischen schwer, Euch das Alles begreiflich zu machen, was natürlich nicht zu verwundern ist, da man sich mal auch ein jüngerer Mensch es nicht fassen kann, das all das, was sich vor unseren Augen abspielt, Wirklichkeit sein soll. Es bleibt einem aber nichts anderes übrig, als sich mit den gegebenen Tatsachen abzufinden. Ich hoffe, dass Ihr in der Zwischenzeit schon so viele Nachrichten von uns erhalten habt, dass Ihr nun nicht mehr besorgt seid. Wir sind alle gesund u. hoffen dasselbe von Euch. Ich hoffe auch bald Nachricht über Greta's u. Peter's Reisepläne zu erhalten. Dass die l. Greta versuchen wird, über die C.S.R. fahren zu können, wäre wirklich sehr gut. Vielleicht werden wir irgendwie einrichten können, nach Wien zu kommen. Darüber weiss ich aber noch nichts Bestimmtes. Ihr werdet rechtzeitig Nachricht erhalten. Was für Ergebnisse zeigen die Bestrebungen der l. Adele, nach der C.S.R. zu kommen. Warum hält sie sich darüber so im Stillschweigen? Bei mir hat sich nichts geändert. Meine Gedanken sind aber nicht mehr hier.

Viele innige Küsse von uns allen! Euer [illegible]

Figure 1.

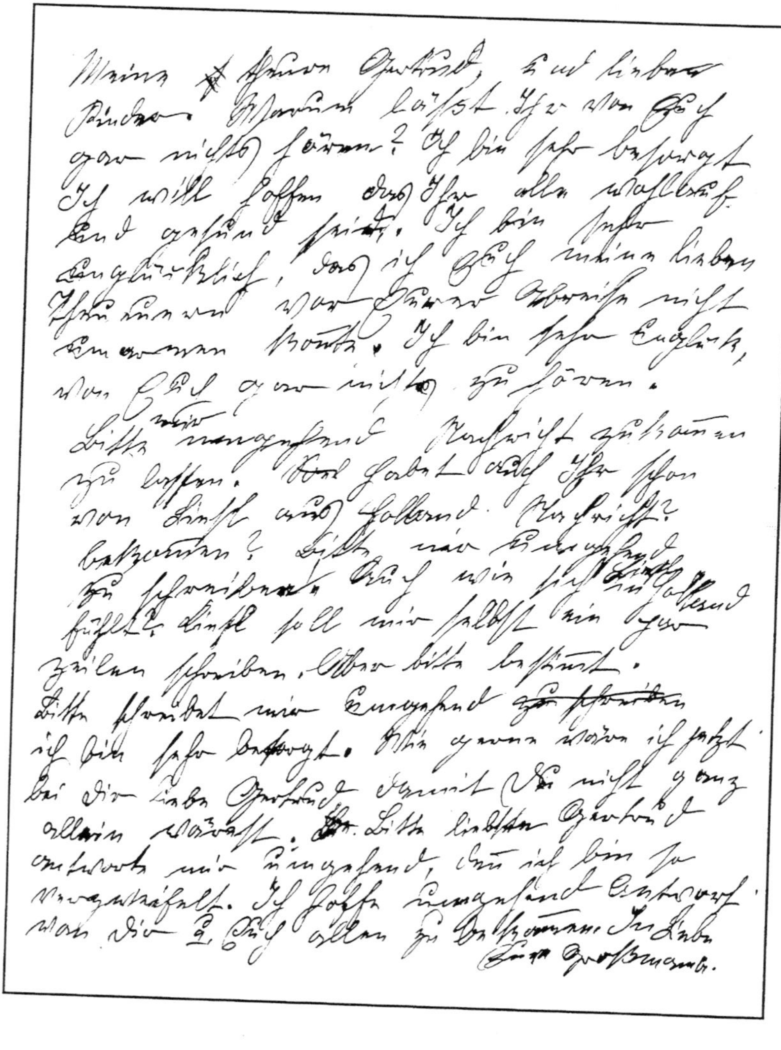

Figure 1a.

Figure 2.

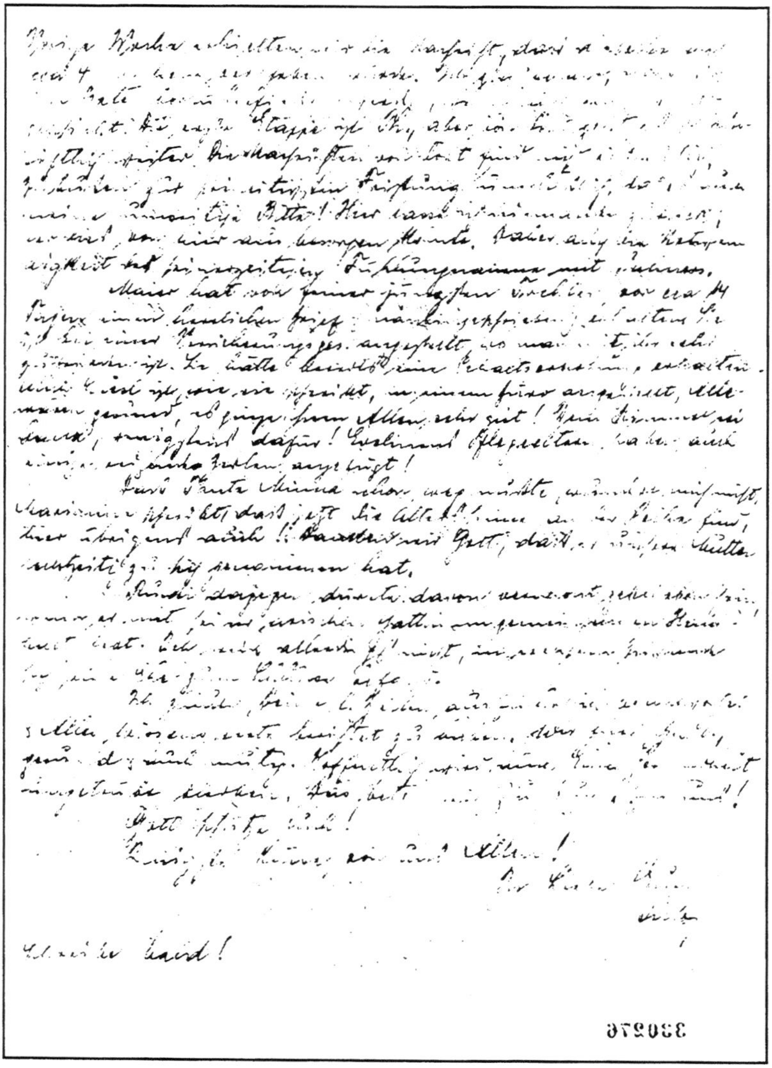

Figure 2a.

Görlitz, 2x/1. 1945.

Meine Liebe!

Nun ist es so weit. Morgen
früh treten wir unsere Reise an.
Ich hoffe, Du hast meinen letzten
eingeschriebenen Feldpostbrief erhalten. Ich teile Dir jedenfalls
nochmals die genaue Adresse mit:

J. P. Franz. Co Nr. 782
K. Post Gar.... (Böhmen).

... nicht an Oskar u. Hans zu
schreiben wegen ....
...... wird besser sein, mir Küster
ein Brot-Packete zu senden, da
ich ja Zoll nicht bezahlen kann.
Bitte ....

870901

Figure 4.

zu machen. Wegen Bedeutung soll er
sich s. an Regiment Angehörige
wenden.

Schreibt fleissig und an vorste-
hende Adresse nur Korrespondenz-
Karten mit kurzem Inhalt. Seid
nicht unruhig u. besorgt, wenn von uns
ev. keine Nachricht, [illegible] wir
in dieser Hinsicht Alles mögliche
tun werden.

Teile auch [illegible] Onkel Fritz
mit, damit Gerta orientiert ist.
Bleibt jedenfalls mit Oskar in
Fühlung!

Wir sind ruhig u. gefasst. Wir
verzweifeln nicht, sondern denken
an dieser Schicksalsschweren

Figure 4a.

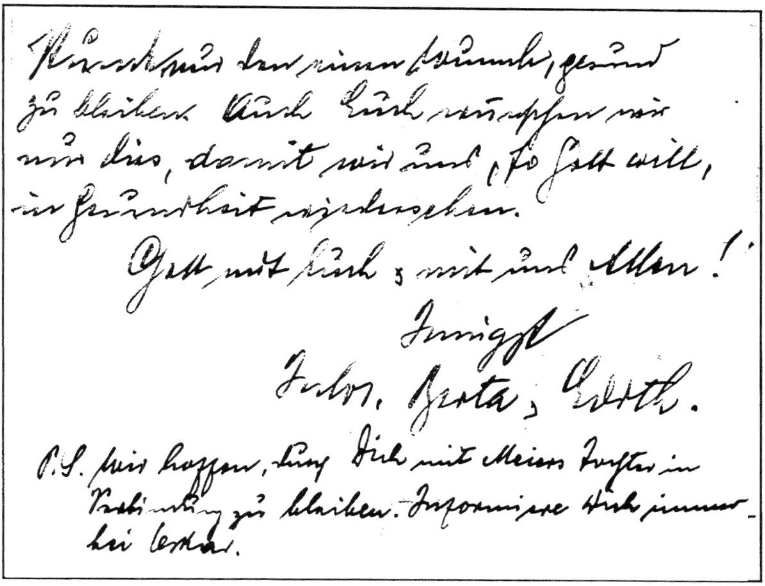

Figure 4b.

Prag, 10/XI. 41.

Meine liebe Adele: Liebe Freunde!

So hat eine treue Seele aufgehört zu sein, ein gutes, treues Herz schlägt nicht mehr. Ich weiss, Adele, was es heisst eine Mutter zu verlieren — und doch glauben Sie mir, ich danke Gott, dass meine Eltern nicht mehr leben. Ihrer guten Mutter ist es erspart geblieben diese schwere Zeit zu begreifen u. so hat sie darunter nicht gelitten. — Ich war gleich nach Erhalt Ihres Telegramms bei der Chevra und

———————————————————

Nochmals unser aufrichtiges Beileid!
Bleibt gesund!
In Liebe u. Freundschaft.
Eure treuen
Empfangen Sie auch von mir
mein innigstes Beileid und viele innigste Grüsse
m. Frau   Ihre Käthe
Mein ältester Bruder der ... u. dem
3.ten Transport weg. Von Hanna u. Peter beiden keine ...
... in 2-3 W. wieder.

Figure 5.

Epilogue

During a recent holiday in South Devon I began to think about writing this last section of my story, and I was made poignantly aware of the sacrifices made by so many in the cause of the war when I saw on Slapton Sands the Operation Tiger Memorial, dedicated by the USA in honour of the men of the US Army's First Engineer Special Brigade, the Fourth Infantry Division and the Seven Corps Headquarters and the US Navy's Eleventh Amphibian Force, who perished in the waters of Lyme Bay during the early hours of April 28th 1944. They were taking part in training exercises in preparation for the Normandy landings, and the inscription ends with the words, 'May all these soldiers and sailors be remembered not only for their sacrifice but also for their contribution to the Allied cause in World War II.'

The gratitude we all owe to these men, some barely more than boys, and countless other brave men and women, can never be adequately expressed, neither can words – least of all mine – truly paint the suffering endured and indomitable courage in the face of inhuman cruelty shown by the victims of Nazism, such as the members of my own family about whom I have written. I myself can never forget them and they often come to me in my dreams. They have never aged. If in reading these pages you gain a better understanding of the times through which we lived and remember the protagonists depicted therein with love and reverence, then maybe I have succeeded by making them live again in your hearts and minds.

September 1995